To Ruth,
love f

CW00471245

About the Author

A dedicated teacher for twenty plus years and counting! Barbara Steel Knowles has lived in Germany, Saudi Arabia and Cyprus and finds inspiration in life's small moments.

Dedication

To my daughter, who changed my life and family and friends who share it.

Barbara Steel Knowles

TOO HOT TO TALK TO A PEANUT

A COLLECTION OF ARTICLES

Barbara Steel Knowles

AUSTIN MACAULEY
PUBLISHERS LTD.

A CIP catalogue record for this title is available from the British Library.

ISBN 978 1 84963 837 1 (Paperback)

www.austinmacauley.com

First Published (2015)
Austin Macauley Publishers Ltd.
25 Canada Square
Canary Wharf
London
E14 5LB

Printed and bound in Great Britain

Well, I'm not walking down there in the searing heat to talk to a peanut

I've lived in Cyprus for a decade and don't want to leave; it feels like home. Cypriot people are charming and charismatic. They are silver-tongued charmers who can convince the toughest cynic that black is white. It depends on your perspective, you see. Viewed in certain lights, the reflective surface of a black object is white. A Cypriot friend helped me realise that.

They are philosophical and resigned to their fate, helpless in the hands of the Gods. "What can we do?" They shrug and accept storm, tempest, personal and financial crisis. Whilst they sometimes make a half-hearted attempt to find the source of the problem their findings are startling and unfathomable.

The ancient freezer in an apartment we rented continually created icebergs which decreased its storage capacity and threatened to throw open the door. My landlord spoke to me patiently, face contorted in earnest. The painful truth was that I had no understanding of domestic requirements. As an English woman who knew that intermittent defrosting is important, I did not appreciate, as all Cypriot house wives do, that you have to do it every other day. In this way the icebergs are held at bay. As he left I muttered apologies for my tardy ways and even thanked him.

During the course of ten years I've gravitated to their way of life although I can't lose the English habit of punctuality which means I spend a lot of time waiting in restaurants on my own.

Some visitors to the island find their attitudes questionable. Things I've grown accustomed to are a source of amazement to them. Anja is fastidious about food and she drives chefs wild. She wasn't prepared for our teenage waiter's reaction to blemished (or muddy; I wasn't sure) cauliflower florets. He sighed and explained, very slowly as you would when speaking to an alien or a foreigner, that it is a Cypriot custom to eat all of the cauliflower; the stalk and the flower. With a shrug of the shoulders he walked away "but MUD..." my niece cried "MUD?" He rolled his eyeballs and retreated into the kitchen saying "What can we do." Well we laughed till we cried, after all, what could we do.

I saw her cross swords many times over food and nutrition. It was exhausting sometimes and I willed her to lower her standards. Peanuts were a source of conflict once. Oblivious to the delights of local almonds, pistachios and walnuts, temptingly piled onto the counter, she chose a packet of peanuts. The assistant assured her they were the freshest of nuts. They sat in the fridge for a week and were opened one 35 degrees Celsius afternoon when I was already over heated and irritable. They were declared soft and rancid which they were. We debated the course of action until I tired of it and binned them "Oh, no", she cried. "They are not fresh and we must take them back". I pointed out how far we'd have to walk and how hot it was but she was indignant and ranted on about the dishonesty of the shop girl until I'd had enough. "Well, I'm not going down there in the searing heat to talk to a peanut!" I cried......and thus the book title of the small moments of my life was born.

"Gone!"

What did she mean, my little daughter, when she said, "Gone!"? The obvious answer was that the word means 'something has disappeared' just as it does in adult language. But obvious answers are rarely the correct ones. The object was perfectly visible to me, but she didn't believe in it. It was transformed because it had broken. Therefore, to her, it had 'gone'. I notice she uses the word a lot. It also describes something that has been put away, or when there's no space for anymore and when the clothes are in the washing machine. It's a mixture of what she perceives and what she believes. She is really expressing quite a sophisticated, abstract notion with this 'simple' word.

Learning to talk is one of the greatest steps in child development. As parents we delight in it. It is a deeply moving and often hilarious experience. We have been enjoying the first words of our daughter, now almost two years old, for several months.

Once the first word is produced others quickly follow. I'm glad I recorded Jasmine's first words since they are now in use every day and have become unremarkable. It is when new words are uttered that I get excited.

They might be single words but they are used as if they were sentences. 'More' means 'I want more'. 'Daddy?' with the voice-stress on the second syllable means 'Where is Daddy?' 'Daddy' repeated as he enters, 'Daddy!' triumphantly is 'There he is!'

All this is pretty amazing. More astonishing is the number of words she understands and responds to. Children understand more words than they ever use. So do adults come to that.

The number of words Jasmine can say increases daily. But despite this great progress it is still noticeably 'child-talk'.

This is probably the cutest period of language development. She charms us with her efforts to say bigger words. There is real communication between us. She has actually been getting what she wants for a long time. By gesture, facial expression and sounds babies make their wishes very clear!

Now she can say words and is beginning to link them I feel less like a purveyor of goodies and unpaid servant. I feel like her companion.

I have started a diary of her language development. It is little more than a list of words at present.

Language is the central point of the difference between human species and all others. Words unite mankind. It is a wonderful mechanism which provides us with some insight of what goes on in our child's mind. Then you really start to feel you can get to know them. They emerge as personalities with ideas of their own.

It must be a frustrating time for a toddler trying to produce the right words. This must be similar to experiencing inability to exchange views in a foreign country because you don't have the means of expression. This has happened to me lots of times. I've had the desire and will to communicate, but have lacked the means.

No wonder then toddlers sometimes express their frustration in tantrums or other 'antisocial' behaviour.

Spoken words can be used positively or to make negative judgments. We have to beware of treating children as curtly as we do some adults. A derisory remark and frequent attempts to correct pronunciation or grammar will make a child feel hurt or angry and less inclined to try to express themselves verbally.

Toddlers don't think before they open their mouths, but parents should. We shouldn't shout at our children, but we do – a bit of volume helps to grab a toddler's attention. The trouble is that shouting stirs them up. On the other hand, if the controlled form of communication some parents use with their children makes me cringe. They talk to their children with every word carefully considered and articulated. It's as if they are giving elocution lessons. Toddlers are so enthusiastic and fun-loving, they need grown-ups around them to behave the same way, even if it does mean we go over the top occasionally and shout.

I used to think I knew a lot about young children when I was teaching. Then we had Jasmine and I realised how little I knew.

One of the most important things I've learned is to bring her up confidently. We can't help noticing how other people do things and the media presents an odd slant on reality, promoting everyday attempts to find perfection. Needless to say nothing is perfect, but you can feel extremely vulnerable, matching your own efforts against other people.

Above all let me enjoy her. Time goes by so quickly. This toddler will slip from this stage to the next before I know it. Toddlers are so full of life and energy, so full of fun, innocent and imaginative, it's one of the most enjoyable stages of childhood. You have to see it as the 'terrific twos' not the 'terrible twos' as some child-experts name this stage. They have more power than sense that's for sure.

We have to recognise this, apply on own common sense. Then we have to go with the flow. If we are to find the strength to provide the 24 hours a day attention they demand we have to develop more relaxed attitudes.

One thing is for sure, time with our children will soon be 'gone'. Children are fun – let's enjoy them.

When To Say No

I have been asking friends for advice and reading a lot about discipline, since my daughter ceased to be a baby and became a toddler. A baby doesn't act with premeditation so there is no such thing as a true behaviour problem. Babies may cry irritably, sleep badly or cling to you like a leech, but they do not think too deeply about what they are doing.

On the other hand, toddlers can certainly behave badly, and my daughter can give Oscar-winning performances of all attention-seeking antics. The question I face now is, 'How much discipline does she need?' Sleep problems have shattered my sanity up to now, so I've been only as firm as needed to keep the peace. Now I'm sleeping more and therefore capable of coherent thinking, I sense new strategies are required to deal with her egoistic behaviour.

Peace and happiness in the home is the prime aim. This family goal is attainable; how to achieve it is debatable. The word 'discipline' carries frightening imagery, yet it is derived from the Latin word 'to learn'. In this sense, if we, as parents, are happy and in control of our lives, then the example we set should be all a child needs in the way of discipline.

It's rarely as simple as that since the example we set is often far from perfect. To err is human and we are caught up in lives of unrealistic expectations ourselves, forced on us from our earliest years by the media and the misrepresentation by many glossy magazines. They hold fast to the idea of perfection, to which many aspire – perfect parenting, homes, personal elegance and so on.

In reality, life is a compromise; there is little that is perfect so we have to accept that we give of our best and try to be flexible. The perfect home-makers, models or decor have been created for a photographic session. They are a marketing image.

Compromise seems as sensible a stand as any in terms of discipline to my mind. I will take the middle-ground position. I've been teaching small children for long enough to know that they are much happier when they know exactly where they stand. Children thrive on consistent limiting and like to know how far they can go. They need to know what you will accept and what you won't tolerate.

In the old days children were disciplined mainly for the comfort of adults. It was believed that parents should be strict with their offspring to ensure they would eventually conform to socially acceptable standards … adult standards!

Then along came Dr Spock and his kind who assured parents that their babies were instinctively sociable. A more easy-going parenting began until it became popular to forget about discipline. You cannot spoil a baby people were told. Giving them comfort at every turn would create confidence and independence in later life.

It's probably this practice that has produced 'Generation X' as the youth of today is so-labelled. If youth has learnt to question the wisdom of its elders it has, so far, found nothing to replace it with. This era is undoubtedly more selfish, more inward looking with the individual out to look after himself, regardless of the effect it has on others. Our society seems to have moved towards the 'me first' mentality.

We expect a lot of satisfaction, fulfilment and pleasure for ourselves. While this is possibly a good goal, too much of the 'me first' mentality is incompatible with the generosity needed to sustain strong relationships.

The number of teenagers seeking 'support' either from drugs, etc., or the help of psychiatrists, and the extraordinary rise in teenage suicides over the last twenty years surely tells us that at the very least here are the results of poor relationships, and of excessive competitiveness.

The new goals are money and materialism and young people want *now* what it took their parents half a generation to achieve. Money is important I won't deny that, but it should not be allowed to run our lives. Relationships matter most.

I have a loving relationship with my little daughter and I know I can sustain it with learning to say no when I must, yet allowing her freedom to develop her personality and to explore her world. In other words I have to deal with her in a way *I* find comfortable and also takes into consideration other people.

After all my 'research' I conclude that common sense, instinctive parenting is good enough. It's tempting to 'give into' her because it's easier and a pleasure to indulge her whims. But common sense tells me it would make neither of us happy in the long run. I don't intend to behave like a 'schoolmarm' towards her, but there are times when saying no demonstrates your love.

Pushed Around The Clock

Like many other people, I'm sure, I often feel oppressed by the intensity of modern life. It seems all go and all pressure. I have always been a forward planner. A friend calls me a control freak. Maybe she has a point, there aren't enough times in my life when I loosen up and allow some time for spontaneity. It makes me uptight and it changes your perspective on life.

Health and sanity require you to surrender the impulse to worry when matters aren't within your control. You cannot be responsible for everything and the sun will rise each day whether you are ready for it or not.

Fortunately, I have a small daughter and life is full of surprises. I recognise that the time she is willing to spend with me will decrease as she grows older and more independent. Thus I seize as many opportunities as possible to play with her and have fun.

Recently I watched a television programme about children with special needs because they are suffering from Attention Defect Hyperactivity Deficit (ADHD). It is a growing problem. These are children who cannot play normally, who are unable to concentrate and who are disruptive because they cannot obey rules. They are often misdiagnosed as naughty children who have behavioural problems. They do have problems because they are often unable to socialise or perform academically, but they are not 'naughty'.

Currently, there appears to be an epidemic of ADHD. Why? Neuroscientists and psychologists are intensively researching the problem. The drug Ritalin has proved a lifeline, but no one knows the long-term effects of this drug. The short-term gain is that ADHD children are less disruptive but one cost is its bad effect on high level creative activity, and there may be other serious, negative effects.

The growing use of Ritalin in the USA (where one in eighteen children use the drug) and the UK, to a lesser extent, has alarm bells ringing for parents and teachers alike. Clearly there has to be an alternative to drug treatment. There are few schools in the USA, which caters to the needs of these children without the use of drugs.

So, what are their needs and why is the problem growing? Studies indicate that it is because there is a conflict between instinct and social behaviour today. ADHD children are those who want to play in the wrong places, at the wrong time.

These days the opportunities and places to play are diminishing. In addition, schools have decreased the time to play. More class-time, at the expense of playtime has increased the numbers of ADHD children. That is indisputable. But the amount of time children are forced to sit at a desk is still increasing. That is happening despite the fact that primary school research has shown that inattention, fidgeting and finger-tapping, etc. increase in proportion to the amount of time children are forced to sit still.

ADHD is more prevalent among boys. That's no surprise since boys seem to need more time for physical activity than girls. However, we humans have a play system in the brain

15

and so do animals. If children are denied the impulse to play they will display pathological behaviour.

One aspect of play is that it teaches social behaviour. We all have to learn socially acceptable behaviours. Children with ADHD need to play more. They crave stimulation. They also need to feel accepted; they usually feel rejected.

The sheer scale of diagnosis raises concerns about the increasing emphasis of performance in society today. In minimising play we are asking for trouble.

Play for adults takes different forms and has different names – sport, socialising, parties, etc. But it all has the same purpose: to help people relate, relax and recharge their batteries. People denied the opportunity to mix with other people in a social setting or to 'let off steam' become unhappy and stressed.

It is strange how we manage to fit into our lives all the things we feel we ought to do – whether we want to or not. Yet we often put obstacles in the way of off-loading some of the demands made on us. But the only way to survive the madness of modern day life is to give ourselves the opportunity to enjoy ourselves sometimes, just for the fun of it, without feeling guilty.

If we really want to change things for the better for our children we need to begin to prioritise our own lives in a very different way. Otherwise one legacy we will give them will be neurosis.

What Are We Doing To Our Children?

I have been a long-time admirer of Shirley Conran, who brought up four children and had a successful career. She is probably most famous for her book *Superwoman*, which gives lots of practical tips to working-mothers. Her advice has apparently enabled a lot of women 'to have it all'; that is, a career and a family life. She wrote, "Life is too short to stuff a mushroom". It could be a philosophy of life for those of us who try to cram too much into our hectic schedules. The most negative aspect of stress is that we transmit it to others. Stressed people tend to affect their spouse and their children.

Recently, in Britain, a conference, *Work-life Balance* was organised by Shirley Conran. Most parents would be horrified to be told that their child was suffering from stress. Stress is for adults, isn't it? Yet there is evidence that this scourge of modern life is affecting the supposedly carefree lives of children. The focus of this conference was young people and stress.

Experts estimate that stress-related illnesses among children have more than doubled in the past twenty years. There is a relentless rise in the number of teenage suicides and growing numbers of young people are being treated for eating disorders and depression. Many bottle up their worries because they are aware of the amount of stress in their parents' lives, and don't want to add to it. Because they have no strategies for dealing with stress the reaction to it can lead to smoking, drugs and fighting.

Many parents are so busy trying not to succumb to stress in their own daily lives that they have no energy for family life. Children require security, encouragement, time – and above all 'a sympathetic ear'; someone to talk their problems through with. These days they are more likely to have mothers juggling the conflicting demands of the workplace and home, and fathers drained by the twelve-hour day.

British parents tend to work a longer week than any other workforce on the continent. They also pay higher taxes, pay more for basic commodities as well as luxury goods and face the highest prices for housing. It is not surprising that an increasingly work-dominated culture is being generated.

It is children, as well as adults, who need to be helped to focus on a work/life balance and to try to find healthy methods of dealing with stress. Instead, neglected offspring are learning a bleak lesson – that life is all work and no play

Today academic pressure is constant. Fewer numbers of children in Britain play sport, enjoy family meals or enjoy a decent family life. We have family members in their teens, who have experienced the pressures of a society obsessed by performance, income and success. They have survived, literally and figuratively, but many of their peers have not. The wellbeing and mental health of the future generation is a matter of great concern. At last, in my country, academics, policy-makers, research experts and caring adults are united in a bid to find solutions to the problems generated by contemporary life.

Sadly, many believe that parents are largely responsible for this state of affairs. It is a bitter paradox that a highly competitive society which puts children under pressure to be successful has simultaneously withdrawn everything they need in order to be successful. Exhausted, over-stressed parents find it almost impossible to deal with children's problems at the end of a tiring day. The effect of this has been to create a distance between children and parents, which was rare in previous generations. Great harm has been done to children through the social changes in the past few decades.

I have a number of friends from many different countries who tell me the problem is not peculiar to Britain. Only a week ago, I read that there have been fourteen child-suicides this year in Hong Kong and the problem is growing. It is a global, 21st century malady and we will all be the losers, children and parents alike, if we do not make time for them in their formative years.

It is unrealistic to be nostalgic about the days when the father went out to work and the mother devoted herself to bringing up the children. But society must find ways to give its young the support and love they need. There are no easy solutions. Countries seem committed to squeezing ever more work from their populations. Little wonder family life is suffering. It is a bitter irony that a generation which has surrendered to the destructive pressures of modern life in order to give their children a better life is in fact creating misery for them. The obsession with success is running out of control, and the race 'to get ahead' will mean that childhood will pass with everyone being the loser.

A Good Night's Sleep

2 a.m. I force myself to stay awake, although I long to sleep. I have had a bad dream and I don't want to drift back into it. It is strange that dreams only last for seconds; they seem to go on for hours, especially when you are experiencing a bad one.

I was dreaming that my teeth fell out in a public place maybe that's because I am going to the dentist's today. However, a dream therapist would interpret it as a subconscious fear that no-one is listening to me. I'd laugh at that; I'm well aware that, at times, no one is listening to me. That's probably because I talk too much!

We are all familiar with the idea that dreams are symbolic but do they really contain solid practical advice that could improve our lives? A psychiatrist would say yes. Dreams can help you solve problems and issues in your life because you are much more honest when asleep, than when you are awake. Dreams are like having a conversation with your subconscious mind, which does not make excuses or repress things. So, dreams can be a valuable tool for resolving your problems.

That's all well and good if you can actually remember them. I rarely remember pleasant ones. Apparently you can train yourself to do so. The trick is to tell yourself, before you sleep, that you are going to recall your dreams when you wake. This way you imprint it on your subconscious mind. If you do wake in the night you write it down. I think I'd be wide awake at this point. The idea that I must remember my dreams would keep me awake for a start. Writing in the early hours of the morning, especially if I'd forgotten to put a pad and pen beside the bed, would ensure I stayed wide awake until it was time to get up.

Understanding dreams has become yet another modern day touchstone. There are a lot of new books on the subject in the bookstores, and people calling themselves dream-decoders have appeared on the scene. There is a universal symbology of dream images to help us decipher our dreams. For example, dreams of death symbolise change rather than death itself.

If you can't find a dream decoder and analysing your dreams is too much trouble, you can turn to the Internet. There is a dream interpretation service called 'The Dream Emporium' so in reality you can spend a lot more time trying to decode your dreams than you do having them!

I don't want to know what my dreams mean since I only remember horrible ones. So I'm probably missing messages from my subconscious. I'm probably too tired to react to them anyhow.

Having a baby daughter who refuses to sleep and who apparently needs so little sleep means I'm not getting much myself. When you are suffering sleep deprivation you think about sleep a lot, as one would be bound to think of water if lost in the desert.

On the plus side, the day seems longer so you can fit a lot into it, and we can stay out late at night, without it upsetting the baby. The downside is feeling weary, and thinking about sleep all the time!

I've talked to a lot of people. It seems girls are often this way; boys tend to be more placid. However, I have a friend with a wakeful baby boy. I wish we lived nearer to each other. We could stay up together!

People talk about sleep as much as they talk about the weather. I've never noticed that before. Apparently, 20% of adults take up to two hours to drop off to sleep. It is thought to be due to the modern pace of life and levels of stress.

I fall asleep immediately when I get the chance but I can't remember what an unbroken night's sleep is like. If only bedtime could be an orderly routine, followed by lights out and silence, instead of a battleground of tears and tantrums.

I'm not surprised sleep-deprivation is used as a 'softening up' process by certain secret police. It is a form of torture; a few more nights of this and I'll confess to anything! Sleep deprivation is easily identifiable from the darkened bags under the eyes, to the weary: defeated stoop of someone who looks as if they've just run (and lost) a marathon.

Theories are all well and good, but when you put them into practice they're disappointing. Ultimately, you have to accept that all sleeping patterns are individual. Some people need ten hours, others, driven individuals thrive on a little as four hours.

An interesting side issue has emerged from all this. The advice given to me by a variety of people puts them in two camps. One group believe multiple disturbances are part and parcel of parenting. The other group maintain you have to be strong and if the baby wishes to cry all night he/she should be left to get on with it.

I've learned a few things about myself too. I know I'm not as tough as I thought. I seem to have left discipline in the school where I taught. I also know I'd give almost anything for a good night's sleep, dreams and all!

A Family Affair

Our family has always been of prime importance to me and my husband. They are the focus of our lives. Because we live abroad we have to make contact constantly and relationships are nurtured with news and caring from afar. We try to do normal things in abnormal circumstances. We regret not seeing as much of all of them as we'd like, but we're lucky and our family ties are strong.

There is concern in our homeland, for the breakdown of family life. The structure is now very different from at any other time in history. Families are very different now because times change and things move on. Many families are under a lot more stress in the modern world in a way they weren't when I was growing up.

More marriages now end in divorce; more children are brought up in lone parent families. Many children never have the experience of the traditional family unit. The stresses of having to juggle the demands of work and family are the biggest problems married women have to face. Working fathers work longer hours often far from the family home; they are not able to spend as much time with their families as they would like.

There are many social issues affecting Britain's families in these ever-changing times. But however different the circumstances, family life is still very much at the heart of all our communities. Most people want, or long for, a strong and stable family life. Young people are no exception. A recent survey of the 'Millennium Generation' found that, while they are ambitious risk-takers in their career goals, they opt for the security of traditional goals in their home life.

They want to be rich, naturally enough and they are ambitious and shrewd. Their optimism comes from their upbringing through years of rising stock markets. They enjoy their leisure hours and are ferociously snobbish about fashionable brands of clothes. But these young adults, both men and women, share the down-to-earth goals of owning their own house and having children. These independent minded youngsters who took Britain into the new millennium have an encouraging combination of ambition and traditional values.

It is particularly encouraging given the findings of a three-year project by the Mental Health Foundation. The report revealed that the breakdown of the traditional family is causing unprecedented levels of mental illness among children. Before they leave the home, a vast number of children will need professional help to overcome problems ranging from mild anxiety to clinical depression.

Some problems are caused by outside factors but failures in the home are often to blame. Divorces, arguments, violence, abuse and inconsistent or unclear basic disciplinary skills are all cited in the report.

More children now have parents under stress, having to cope with several things at once, both at home and at work. These parents may be able to provide more materially to their children than mine were able to, but at what a cost.

The problems are linked to changes in society, but the family is fundamentally important. A lot of the causes are directly linked to problems in the family. Disruptive disorders could be caused by genetic factors and parental failure. I spent a long, long time in a European airport recently waiting for a delayed plane. Along with other mothers and their children I found the waiting annoying and worrying. The wait-time seemed interminable and became very stressful when a family arrived with two badly-behaved youngsters who were allowed to do exactly as they liked. They pleased themselves by running about screaming, interfering with other passengers' food and belongings, trashing the seats, spilling drinks and so on and on and on! At one point their mother turned to me with a radiant smile, and said, "I can't do a thing with them. They are hyperactive." Nice excuse to sit back and do nothing, I thought. 'Hyperactivity' the modern tag for simply bad behaviour and lack of discipline. Disciplining children is hard work and it is the parents' responsibility. Too often the job is left to teachers in school and often their hands are tied, because the parents don't want their child to be upset. A child told off in the loving security of a good home is less likely to be upset. All children *need* the security of a firm code of behaviour, whether they seem to like it or not! How else can they learn consideration for others, which is a life skill that helps us all live in harmony.

It's unrealistic to blame the government. Certainly they have to provide the funds to deal with the problems young people are facing, and to support parents with financial difficulties. But they cannot turn off the television and talk to their children for you, nor take them for walks pointing out all the interesting things along the way. The interests of children should be right at the heart of family life.

I asked my teenage niece her views on the ideal family life. I think she summed up what we all want when she said the family should be a special place where you can be totally natural and remove your social mark. It's where things that need doing are done out of love; and no one counts the cost.

Love is what family life is all about. It's shelving your own needs and tending to those of the younger (or older) generation. The animal kingdom manages it very well; we can too!

Father, Mother ... Friend

Our family reunion this summer was a happy affair. We gathered three generations from across England, from as far away as America and the Middle East. Grandmothers, fathers, mothers, sons and daughter, cousins, uncles and aunts met up for a week-end at the seaside; Teens to twenties, middle-aged and elderly shared news, views and dreams ... of the future, of the past.

For all of the doom and gloom about the future of the family most of our contemporaries are making greater effort to stay in touch with their extended family. People are enjoying affable and easy relationships, irrespective of age. Little is off limits conversationally and as the young are free spirits, the older generations young-at-heart, real friendships can emerge from kinship; all the confessionals and discussions are bonding.

During the past thirty or forty years, a more democratic and amicable relationship has developed between parents and their children. Parents have become real people with feelings and failings, so there's more shared ground.

Children's lives are much more bound up with their parents than they used to be. In the past parents were shadowy but significant figures in the background. Modern parents are part of an ongoing process of adjustment from minder to mentor and hopefully, finally, friend.

However, it is important to realise when we might be making an unwanted intrusion into their territory. We need to maintain a balance so there is a sufficient gap between the generations. Parents need to know when to back off and accept that we are the older generation.

A lot of parents feel excluded when their children are in the process of pulling away, partly because they're fearful for them. But growing up is about making your own mistakes. Children should be able to feel they have a secure place in their parent's hearts and minds but they need their privacy too. We don't need to know every detail of their lives to ensure their safety.

But it's a tightrope we tread; we have to demonstrate the exact degree of attention. Too much is translated as over-anxiety or lack of trust, lack of privacy and so on. But we make them feel undervalued, insignificant and that we are uncaring or indifferent if we show too little!

And they need us to share information regarding our future plans even though all you get from them is a grunt. We recently experienced what felt like role reversal when we earned the disapproval of number two son for not giving him enough details regarding our holiday arrangements.

Conversely, liberal households where children are privy to all the anxieties and concerns and where there are no areas that are off limits are stifling and stressful. It's a heavy burden for children to carry; they do not want to know all the bad and sad things in their parents' lives. Deep down they want to go out and have fun feeling that everything is fine at home.

Being parents doesn't mean you can't meet children as equals in some respects, but it does mean remaining on an adult level emotionally. At times they need us to exercise some authority and objectivity. That is their touch-stone, their security zone.

It means being prepared to be unpopular sometimes; even though everyone wants to be liked there are times when you have to say 'no' regardless of their displeasure or dislike. Nowadays there are so many parents dealing with their children in such personal and informal ways they find it impossible to be firm with them. They are so compulsively centred on giving the child what it wants that saying 'no' has become impossible.

Ultimately, those children who are indulged often become over-demanding and unpleasant. This kind of indulgent relationship won't matter when they grow up. They will only come and see you when they've left home if they like you ... and they will only like you if they have respect for you.

Our family meets together because we like each other; we like doing things together. We're good friends. Those friendships grew from bonds created through family values and mutual respect. "As you sow, so shall you reap."

A Mother's Touch

Its 6:00am bright sunshine beams through the thin curtains, waking me. I turn over and try to go back to sleep, but my cosy bed, the duvet I happily snuggled into last night is stifling. It's too warm and the insistent calls of wood pigeons in the garden drive me from my bed.

I make coffee, moving as quietly as I can, for I am the only one awake and creep into the summer room. I always think of it as the summer room this glass extension built on to my Mother's home although she sits in there every morning of the year watching the birds in the garden.

Sunlight dances on the patchy shadows on the grass, the trees sway in the breeze against an azure-blue sky. The noisy wood pigeons, daring in the quiet of the day, swoop down to steal nuts from the bird-house; they are plump and content. Bobbing up and down on the lawn, sparrows hungrily peck insects and then fly off to some secret retreat. More birds sit in the trees calling to each other, swinging to and fro on breeze-blown branches.

My Mother's flower garden is a riot of colour, full blooms at the height of their beauty, familiar flowers, English flowers; the flowers of my youth. The pictures I carry in my mind when I am far away are of my Mother in her garden, which she loves so much and where she works hard. Memories of her nurturing seeds, creating new life and housing bulbs and plants from the winter cold are constant. I remember the house always filled with flowers in the summer, some bought, some given, she always seemed to be surrounded by flowers. In the winter, sheltering plants were everywhere; none abandoned to the cold, they perched on every surface; cupboards, tables, every kitchen appliance held plants, window ledges from bedroom to bathroom stacked with plants. You had to look where you were walking; floor space was invaded by plants, moving from room to room, an obstacle course. Although this invasion was sometimes inconvenient, irritating, the care of her plants, her devotion to their wellbeing has always been symbolic to me of her love and concern for us. We are blessed with mother-love which has been our strength and good fortune throughout our lives.

Wherever I am, I feel closer to my mother in a garden than anywhere else on earth. The garden I am looking at now is a far cry from my own. Here the flowers and plants are demanding, needing almost constant attention, They need water, but hate torrential rain, must have sun or must have shade, need to be moved, need more space ... They are sensitive and want constant attention; perhaps they remind her of her children!

I love this time with my mother. It's the school holidays, long, seeming endless in this timeless zone before my husband joins me. Before we begin our hectic schedule fitting in all the things we like to do together during his short holiday period. I am spending time with my mother ... I have gone from a busy, sometimes frantic pace of life to a quiet existence, a lazy time when my only decision in the day is what to have for lunch.

This is not my household to organize and keep running. I offer help, of course, but it is not my responsibility, they are not my problems. So this is where my mind runs free, this is where I relax and rest. I have time; time to sit and stare, time to reflect, to dream. The tight knot of tension within me uncoils; I relax and I am free.

Worth more than gold these precious days; few people are this lucky. Few people have the time to be so self-indulgent. Not many people have such a place to go, or such a mother to go to. It is as if I become a child again. My life becomes undemanding and stress free I don't contact or see people, except by chance. This is my retreat and I emerge refreshed in spirit and charged with energy. It is therapy for mind and body.

Therapy appears to be the buzz word in England at present. Every newspaper, every magazine I pick up carries an article relating to stress-relieving therapy. In an attempt to improve physical and mental well-being, therapy is being introduced into the workplace and the home. Industry, personal and management, artisan and professional, even medical practices are seeking help. Changes in lifestyle and values have brought about the disintegration of family and community. People are looking into themselves for solutions. More and more people are doing so with the help of a therapist. The variety of therapies available is suddenly endless ranging from psychotherapy, hypnotherapy, family therapy, rigorous physical treatment and behavioural therapy to counselling, and group therapy.

It is big business, costly and difficult to assess. It is being hailed as the antidote of modern life; a panacea for all ills. The problem with the rise of the therapy culture is that it is also the rise of victim culture. It is born out of a fascination with 'self' the danger is that it abandons a sense of the outside world. What we really need from any therapy is personal healing, which will serve to improve our lives and the effect we have on life and those around us.

Solitary, self-indulgent, self-expression can be negative and defeating. It can lead to people blaming the world and everyone else for their problems. When talking releases feelings and things best left unsaid it can do no good. If you look to America where some people have been in therapy for decades it seems to have created more unhappiness and perpetuated the troubled soul.

What we all seek is a little time to ourselves; time out for a relaxing recreation, a time to pause for thought, to re-learn to shield ourselves from stress with humour.

It's all here in my mother's house. However, as she's just read this article, she wishes to point out that this therapy is available only to close members of the family!

Role Reversal

While today's teenagers and twenty year olds tend to regard their parents as people who are past their sell-by-date, they are not actually concerned with the idea of looking after them. That time will come, although there is no way of knowing how society will deal with the aging percentage of the population by then.

The problem now faces people in their fifties – what do we do with an aging mother and father? The decision is often reached later in life these days because people are, in general, more active and healthier for longer. Older people do not have to give up their independence as soon as they did in the past. They drive their own cars, go on lots of cheap out-of-season holidays, go hiking and join a lot of clubs.

Every celebration or family gathering is enriched by their presence. Each age-group enjoys their company, stories, selfless affection and enviable lack of inhibitions. Many youngsters prefer their grandparents' company to that of their parents. Somehow the age-gap bridges any difficulties and creates a relaxed, easy relationship. It is probably true that many grandparents have a more enjoyable time with their children's' offspring than they did with their own. The fact that they can go off to their own peaceful home whenever they like must help!

In most cases though, there comes a time when bodies become frail or illness attacks and the aged have to surrender their independence. Then they are struck with fear – either at having to go into a residential home, or the thought of living in a home with teenagers. Most old people would prefer to live in their own home.

But when it is no longer possible, and there is no money to pay for residential care, then their children take them into their homes. There will come a time when a lot of middle-aged people are stuck between a rock and a hard place. They haven't finished bringing up their own families when they are obliged to be responsible for their parents. When there are siblings families often share the 'burden'. Mum, or dad, stay at different homes for varying lengths of time – a sort of human pass-the-parcel. Yet it is probably the best option, giving everyone 'space' and a change of outlook.

I don't know the exact time when the metamorphosis takes place – the moment when the child becomes the parent and the parent becomes the child. It varies but everyone with grown children faces the pressure. When they simply mislay something and the children look at them with that 'Mum-is-losing-her-memory-look', and so on. I went to stay with my mother for an extended period, for family reasons, and nearly drove her crazy by 'looking after her'. My intentions were good but she is not ready to 'let go of the reins'. I am still the child in her eyes and she is fit enough, thank God, to run her own life.

Life has changed for old people over the last few decades. It is as much due to a change in attitude as health. Few people now retire with the intention of pottering around in the garden, or spending their days glued to the television. No! They are out and about visiting new places, learning new skills, starting new hobbies. There are seventy and eighty year old marathon runners who could give most of us a run for our money!

They are an inspiration and a hope for the future. Young people may think life is over when you hit your thirties. There are plenty of older folk who know that it is not.

The time comes however, when we start to feel protective towards our own parents. They may find it irritating, but it seems to be a human instinct. There is no place in time when it occurs, it just happens. It amuses me to see how number one son, now 22 years old, tends to mentally drive for his father on family outings. He used to be happy to bounce about on the back seat. Now he is in the front, beside his father driver, and he is the one doing the back-seat driving not me!

It is suggested that our short-term memory degenerates as we grow old. People joke about it… 'You know you are getting old when you stoop to tie your shoelaces and wonder what you are doing down there', etc. Maybe it is a bonus from Mother Nature. We return to a younger frame-of-mind when we remember only the things we want to. We realise that all the things people worry about forgetting do not really matter.

Now that is a thought. It must be nice to have a mind that is not cluttered and have space to store the important stuff. You get older and memory capacity has to be more selective. I spend half my days mentally sifting through meaningless data to get to the important memory. For the young, and the old, recall is much more immediate. It must be good to focus on fine memories and have the time to share them...

A Death in the Family

My uncle Tony died after a minor operation some time ago. It was an untimely death and a great loss to the whole family. No one read about it in the headlines since he'd never invented anything, or made movies, nor amassed a huge fortune. He was a truly good man, but that rarely makes the headlines. He was ill-paid for the hard work he did for most of his adult life. But he gave to his family riches that money can't buy. His greatest pleasure was his family life; the household was filled with light and laughter, joy and caring. He left a legacy of love.

Many old people worry that they might outlive their money; that they will have nothing left to leave behind. I cannot understand why a parent would feel they have to leave anything for their children. I don't expect anything … for what; for being a daughter?

The only things a parent owes a child are stability, gentleness and love. The kind of love that is constant during bad times and good.

My beloved father died when he was 53 years of age. What he left to me, is still with me and will be all the days of my life … his love. In my life, even in the most trying times for him – and there were a few when I really tested his love – I never felt, ever, that he wasn't there for me with all his heart. I miss him and not a day goes by without me thinking of him or sharing a memory of him with someone.

Everyone misses him. He was a gentleman and a gentle man. He owned several shops in a small town and he was everybody's favourite. He was everyone's favourite friend, everyone's favourite employer, everyone's favourite neighbour. He didn't have an enemy in the world. Everyone called him 'Cheerful Charlie'. You could rely on Dad to brighten any gloom. He was fun and he was also caring and generous and good. We all share so many vivid memories, still feel contained by his love; all this he left to us.

I've watched a number of people at funerals and I am always intrigued as to what they consider a legacy. They talk of what 'Mum' or whoever, would have wanted them to have – silver dishes, some china, jewellery perhaps … and money, there's always the possibility of 'get rich quick'.

Bitter quarrels, greed and envy sometimes emerge in families where people feel the legacy has been divided unfairly. Some disagreements end in the courts where it is left to an impartial judge to sort things out. We can only speculate what the deceased would have thought of that.

. Maybe the Ancient Egyptians had the right idea … Take it with you when you go. After all the survivors are left with the greatest of gifts: *life*.

The county in which I grew up in England had more than its fair share of eccentrics. Many of these were old people who lived alone in trying circumstances. They lived very frugally, in spartan homes, and were renowned for their meagre housekeeping and shabby clothes. But the majority of these people left fortunes.

They denied themselves the most basic of comforts in order to leave great wealth behind. Most pitiful were the obituaries which revealed that the old person, having existed at subsistence level, had left their money to a cat's home, or the like.

Perhaps a pet animal was their only comfort, the only thing on which they devoted affection and received it back. How very sad. However, we express it, love is what we all need.

I don't believe 'All You Need is Love' as the Beatles sang. Only when you are very young do you believe that. We become more practical later – out of necessity. It's no use telling your kids you love them if they are hungry, cold and ill-clothed.

The love I'm talking about isn't on a greetings card. It's working hard when you want to quit; it's giving without looking for any return; it's knowing when to talk and when to be silent: A thousand things.

I never doubted that my father loved me. He was not a demonstrative man and he never said it. But I knew that he did. He was a sick man, but you would never have known it by the effort and the hours he gave to his business. He was determined to give us the best, to give us the things he'd never had. We were his family and we meant all the world to him. He was my champion, my friend and my hero. I miss him, but I don't miss his love, because it is still with me.

Deja Vu

I walked into my classroom, started to ask one of my mischievous pupils to behave and stopped mid-sentence. My mother's voice echoed in my head; the tone of my voice, the very words, were hers. Memories flooded back, from a time when the roles were reversed and I was the naughty child.

I take note through the following weeks; sure enough my mother's expressions which I thought I'd forgotten, came tumbling from my mouth. No doubt I have the same 'certain look' in my eyes that she had when I'm displeased. I see my pupils exchange looks as we did when Mum's eyes flashed.

If you want to know how a woman will turn out, just take a look at her mother. Irritating though that seems to a modern, individualistic woman it does happen women become their mothers!

Once we've struggled through the gawky, uncertain periods in our lives, we develop our own sense of style. Our persona, the way we walk, talk and laugh belongs to us alone. Then slowly, but surely, we change. It becomes more pronounced as the years go by. You start to look like her; laughter lines around the eyes, the same smile and, if you are lucky, cheeks as soft and silky as a baby's. You look in the mirror and there she is, not as she is now, but the way she looked when you first began to see her as a person.

When that happened, we were young women enjoying the adventure of self-discovery. Just as we were intensely self-critical, so we criticised our mothers. We secretly vowed never to wear pink lipstick, a practical raincoat or cosy dressing-gown. Nor would we ever be seen without eye make-up. There was no way we were going to end up as a housewife; we were going to be different.

We rebelled against her conventional ways, resented her advice thinking she knew nothing of the real world or youth. You can't pass on your experience, daughters have to make their own mistakes and a mother has to watch them. My friend says she'll have her revenge once her teenage daughter has teenagers of her own. She's right; the times may change but all mothers share the same concerns about their daughters.

We fight hard against our mothers in order to become adults. But for most women increasing maturity and experience brings the growth of sympathy and compatibility with their mothers. Much of the disharmony between mothers and daughters is due to a difference in lifestyle and youth's indifference to materialism. But it's easy to despise material possessions when you don't have many. Later on, when you have your own home you realise why your mother was so worried about having things damaged or broken.

So when you find yourself turning into your mother, in reality, it is maturity. This is not just a woman-thing either; you notice little by little your man is becoming like his dad. And 'number one son' at 20 years, admitted to doing things his father does to a degree that is, quote, 'Scary'.

My own mother sweetens with age like a good apple. She's the kindest, most thoughtful person I've ever met. Everyone loves her and knows they can depend on her. If that's what I've got to look forward to then I will look in the mirror and smile.

Timeless

At the end of each day I have a number of tasks outstanding. I always seem to run out of time.

Time management is one of my major concerns. But if I can believe all I read, another problem is solved; now you can book a life-coach to make the most of your precious time. It was over a decade ago that the concept of a life-coach was introduced in the United States. New innovations and all manner of techniques to avoid doing things for yourself are definitely in vogue nowadays. It came as no surprise to read that you can train as a life-coach 'virtually', via conference calls to America.

Apparently life-coaching is an 'action-based method of changing things for the future'. Those were the very words in the advertisement placed by a life-coach in a popular women's journal. Just as a personal trainer keeps you motivated to reshape your body, a life-coach focuses on improving your professional and personal life. A coach helps you make the most of your precious time ...

By golly, if I can do that with a couple of phone calls a lot of problems can be solved! Everyone has a different agenda but all of us want more time. It comprises of lists of things to do at home, at work or 'at play'. (I won't call it 'free time' because no one has free time anymore.) I have my own agenda; things I have to do, things I want to do and things I should do.

There's no point imagining what I'd do if I had time because I don't have it. What really perplexes me is the memory of my grandmother who did everything from washing, cooking, gardening to rearing five children without machines to help her. She didn't make lists to prioritise her jobs. She just got on with them and still found time to sit alone in a park or garden sometimes. She would go off to find 'a bit of peace and quiet'. We'd call it 'personal space' or the like, these days. Her house was sparkling clean, her children were well-cared for and the food was fabulous. She did her own baking and there was no such thing as 'take away' food.

So why is it with all the machines we have to do the washing, clean the house, wash the pots and streamline work in the kitchen we never have any spare time? I don't think it's mismanagement of time on my part. Perhaps it is because my grandmother was never offered the distraction of entertainment and the opportunity to do a lot of the things we take for granted as part of life such as working outside the home or socialising.

If I stuck to a routine like she did I'd probably accomplish a lot more. But, the telephone rings and I chat, or someone invites me to lunch or to shop and I readjust my agenda. Today's jobs become tomorrow's chores, or are indefinitely postponed.

So I probably do need a life-coach. Maybe, I could train to be one. No, I haven't time! What I really need to do is to change some of my habits and stop caring about what I think I 'should' be doing. Those things make up most of the clutter in life. I really have no sense of where my time goes. The largest block of my time used to be taken up from the time I left for work until the time I returned home. I no longer go out to work and my time is largely devoted to my daughter.

The decision to stay at home or go out to work is being faced by increasing numbers of wives and mothers. Once that choice has been made it's rarely the end of the matter. The grass is always greener on the other side. Mothers who work outside the home feel over-worked and guilty about their children. Those who stay at home sometimes feel bored.

Certainly the changing role of women in most societies has presented us with more opportunities and more problems than any other time in history. It seems that the idea that we can have it all – home-life, a career and a social life – is the greatest myth of the 21st century.

What we lose out on is the opportunity to spend any time alone. Whether it's time to do nothing, read a book, pursue a hobby or sport we don't have it. If you wait and see if a free evening appears of course it doesn't.

The problem is not peculiar to women. There are plenty of men who work all day and have to attend to routine matters like bill-paying or DIY at home. On top of this a lot of men act as unpaid drivers to their wives and children.

Maybe choice is also a 'time-monster'? We have so many things to choose to spend our time doing. And there is the greatest time-eater of all times, the television. Convenient and undemanding, it lurks in almost every lounge, consuming hours and the willpower to turn it off.

Don't misunderstand me. I'm not anti-TV. Many of the programmes are entertaining or informative. Maybe television's greatest charm lies in the opportunity for mindless space which is the last thing we'd ask for in the midst of our busy, stressful lives – and probably what we need most of all.

Boys to Men

I holiday in England ... the prospect was not too inviting given the bleak, unseasonal weather this spring. But we went, because that is where our families are. We take every possible opportunity to catch up on family news and to see the boys' rapid change and growth every few months. I would not have the temerity to use this term to these youths of eighteen and twenty, but they will ever remain 'the boys' to us.

We were sharing a family meal when it hit me, when I suddenly realised they were boys no more. Eating out is one of the few things we enjoy together. Our young men are no strangers to zoos, swimming, playing games and our taste in movies. So having meals together have become the one certain option...

He hunched over the plate, hair brushing the edge, narrowly missing the dollops of tomato-ketchup. It was a familiar sight, a student's single-minded assault on food. It's pointless trying to get a word out of him when he's eating. This hearty youth who used to peck at a few chicken nuggets or nibble a burger. Finished, he pushed the plate away. He looked up and I saw a mirror-image of his Father, the gentle smile, the quick glance to check he had our attention before he started to speak. He talked of the future, his future; with such confidence and vigour it startled us. Where did he go that boy; carefree and happy-go-lucky teenager?

His brother joins in the conversation. He is younger, less certain, but sure of one thing; he is going to make his own decisions.

It's not easy being with nascent adults, nor is it good for one's self esteem. Parents, previously the recipients of unconditional love are now perceived to be the older generation and out of touch with their world. My husband and I share memories of clashes with our own parents and find to our horror, that history repeats itself.

They want to flex their muscles and our values are frustrating to them. But we are concerned to share our experiences, determined they won't make the same mistakes as we did. The words fall on deaf ears, the annoying demands of people of another generation.

We see them frequently and we are always greeted with a change – of style, hair length, musical taste, and more importantly personal growth. Each time we have adjustments to make, in terms of that growth and a relationship to establish on a different footing.

We have reached a delicate plateau of compromise and wary respect for each other. It's good to realise they like being with us.

The younger boy talked of his interview at University. He is eloquent, entertaining, light years away from the teenage grunt that meant both 'yes' and 'no'. He has become a man, I thought. Throughout the evening he displayed new maturity; he actually said thank you for the meal.

His brother listens to him; he is kinder, almost paternal. They have always fought and argued in recent years; the younger seething with indignation, feeling patronised by his brother. Now they are re-building their relationship, developing respect for each other. They might even become friends once they've passed through the twilight zone betwixt youth and man.

When we are away from them our lives are uncomplicated by their social lives; their chauffeuring and catering needs. We are not disturbed by their loud, incomprehensible music. The refrigerator is never empty and we have time to pursue our own interests but when we say goodbye, we immediately begin to long for the next bout of family life.

Temper, Temper

It was a cheese sandwich that did it ... triggered off my bad-temper. There was nothing wrong with it, nor did I especially want a meat one, but I wanted to be given the choice. I admit I was already grumpy and over-tired after a fourteen-hour flight, but it irritated me to have a cheese sandwich thrust at me by a flight stewardess whose interest in me was so minimal; she pushed it into the book I was reading. With a flash of temper which startled my sister, who was travelling with me, I demanded a meat sandwich. Petty, I know, but sometimes I get so fed up with mass-travel. I feel I should stand in line and bleat like a sheep, passive and faceless.

Anyhow, the meat was horrible, so that served me right, said my sister. I ate the bread and cheered up. We all go through different moods every day. Moods are influenced by shifting tensions and energy levels throughout the day. It's not unusual to feel bad-tempered on waking but raring to go by noon, loads of energy and little stress leads to a good mood. Conversely, when you're tired and have a pile of work to do you're likely to be in a bad mood, though there are people who thrive on overwork. These types are moody when they feel they haven't enough to do.

We meet people in bad moods in every area of our lives. What makes them bad-tempered and unpleasant? Mostly we ignore them. Sometimes we confront them, but in general, we regard this ill-feeling as a feature of living in the 90's. There is no indication that material comfort has brought any feeling of well-being to the 21st Century. People are cranky, stressed, too busy, irritable and rude.

I stood plastic-poised at a cash point the other day, only to be muscled out of the way by a woman with a rucksack, which nearly took my head off. When I protested, she growled that she was in a hurry and went on to tap into every function the machine could perform. There are times to stand your ground but this wasn't one of them. I'm not easily intimidated, but the force of her aggression kept me quiet.

At the airport our innocuous question, "Does this bus go to Terminal B?" met with a snarl, "Can't you read?" and the airport official hurried angrily away – no doubt to complain about demanding passengers.

There are establishments where people are paid to make life easier for you. There, rudeness cuts you to the quick; but you're paying for this! Meeting "I'm too good for this job types" haughty sales assistants, aloof waitresses, offensive clerks one starts to imagine there's a national group operating clandestine customer – abuse courses!

Usually these encounters don't matter in the great scheme of things. But they serve to make one feel angry and resentful. You can knuckle down and accept rudeness, but at some point you will explode. Someone close to you will get the flak or you will explode internally and rage to yourself that you've let someone stamp all over you again. Then one day you will have a mega-explosive reaction to a minor incident, but it will be the culmination of all the instances of rudeness you have suffered, and people will be amazed and alarmed. There are even books on the market designed to help you deal with rudeness and remain in control, so people won't get away with it.

The other side of the picture is painted for me by friends who work in Service areas; sales assistants, taxi-drivers, doctors, telephonist, etc. From their perspective the Public is a seething mass of fury. Discontent is expressed in ill-temper, bad manners, and irrational, even violent behaviour. Some firms have been clever enough to train their staff to disarm irate customers. They centre on the philosophy that there is no such thing as a rude customer, only a person who is behaving badly because of the way they have been treated in the past. Good luck to them. The people they are dealing with will surely leave the encounter in a better mood. With this philosophy they are able to bring out the best in people.

Today we favour emotional openness to the stoic decorum of the past. But there is no indication that people are any happier for self-expression. Perhaps the key to it all is laughter. We take ourselves and each other so seriously these days...

At this point, I hope the rude man in charge or the one and only lounge at the Charles de Gaulle airport and who ordered me and my sister out, because we were not first class passengers, has recovered his equilibrium. He had not anticipated our response and he certainly lost his cool when we laughed and laughed at his pomposity and the stupidity of it all ... an international airport which did not offer a place to rest to all travellers.

As we had to spend seven hours in transit prowling boring gift shops and drinking unwanted coffee in order to sit down, with fourteen hours of travel behind us, the laughter was probably hysterical. But it released our tension and put us in a better mood ... which was just as well as our flight was delayed!

Mirror, Mirror...

Ouch! I've just been plucking my eyebrows. I pause to renew the will to finish the job. It's a pain both literally and figuratively speaking. Hair grows so quickly here, it's a constant battle to keep it in check. I confounded my husband a while ago by refusing to lunch with him because I had to tame my eyebrows. And no, I wouldn't come out before I'd done so. It's OK for a man to sport bushy brows but a 'no-no' for a woman to let nature take its course. They symbolise someone who has 'let herself go'. This norm has been imposed by women, perpetuated by them and so we have to face the consequence – discomfort!

My mother is short-sighted. She can't see her eyebrows without her glasses and they are an obvious obstacle to tweezers. A magnifying mirror helps but can't entirely solve the problem. The professional beauty therapy I treated her to resulted in uneven brows and her refusal to go out for two weeks.

Anyhow, now lunch is no longer on the menu, I may as well get on with my brows... I can't because I need to find the tweezers again. I have this really good pair which I put down when the telephone rang. I can't do without them. There are three places they could be. Beside the 'phone, in the bedroom or my bathroom. Naturally they are not by the 'phone, that would have been too good to be true.

I glance around the bedroom and retreat quickly. It's a scene of chaos since I always pack months before going on leave and this was the day I'd decided to do it. The bed is strewn with clothes, there are more rejects hanging on wardrobe doors, others I've discarded, lie in heaps on the carpet. I haven't a thing to wear. I won't tell my husband as his response is predictable. He will either look at me as if I'm crazy or become angry at my greed. OK, I know it's not literally true. But the truth is I've nothing (I like) to wear today. My instinct is to tip them upside down to find the tweezers I think may be there, and dump the lot.

I resist the temptation and go into my bathroom. I stare hard willing them to appear. All I find is food for thought. Everything I really need in there would fit into a medium-sized bag. So why is it the drawers are stashed with so many make-up bags? Tweezers type objects bulge against the sides, which tantalise me, but it transpires they are nothing more than old lipsticks and eyeliners.

I peer hard at everything and go into a trance. In this state I clear all the surfaces of bottles, jars, boxes and sprays. I empty the drawers of a bewildering array of beauty products. I will banish all this clutter. None of this will happen without my tweezers. I must have neat brows to tackle this lot.

I look in the mirror. They're untidy alright. So is the rest of the villa. I see so clearly now, gazing into the mirror, letting my mind wander round our home. Everywhere is the clutter of our belongings; things we have collected over the years. There are objects we have been unable to resist in shops, and gifts from friends and family. Some things are loved, some I'm indifferent to, I don't even see them any more in this 'mish-mash' of materialism. I fondly imagined it was homely, in fact, it is plainly untidy.

I will have a clear up. I will sort and discard, rearrange and minimalise. Life will be easier. I will find things more quickly and, when I do mislay something, finding it won't involve turning the place upside down.

Leaving the bathroom I head for the lounge. Inspired, I gather everything into the centre of the room ... photographs in frames, bric-a-brac, ornaments, collections of miniature boxes, silverware and pictures. I handle each piece; every one holds a memory for me. I remember how each one of us, her children, have urged my mother to put away some of her 'treasures'. She has always responded by saying, "I could tell you a story about them all". And she did, and so the opportunity to reduce her hoard would pass. So it has continued through the years and we have compounded the situation by giving her souvenirs of our travels. Thus, she has a home bursting at the seams.

I return to my task with determination. I work hard until I have achieved what I had in mind. The exercise is effective. Thinking more clearly now I've minimised this jumble, I remember I left my tweezers in the kitchen. Now, if I could just find my hand mirror ... !

The Emperor's New Clothes

We were watching one of the many fashion shows on the television when my husband turned and asked "Is he joking? Or is he a crook?" He was referring to the designer of the creations we were seeing. If women believe his clothes are attractive they are deluding themselves. There was nothing beautiful or appealing about the clothes or the way the models had been presented.

These bizarre garments were draped around the models, pinned and tucked so they would (possibly) stay in place. The designer had 'experimented' with fabrics, bleaching them either to fade or disintegrate them in places. There was the casual gushing, effusive, mad remarks from the commentators as these travesties of apparel appeared. The Models had their hair tortured into outlandish styles, their skin was whitened and their eyes blackened, so they resembled creatures from a horror story or your worst nightmare. These were lovely, young women degraded by a designer's whim.

More astonishing than the clothes they design is the hype that surrounds 'the new designers'; their colleagues, people who attend the shows on the behalf of consumers – fashion buyers and fashion reporters are ecstatic in their reviews. The designers, when interviewed have a nervous intensity, they talk about the kind of issues that tend to come from academics rather than creators of fashion. They always seem a little weary, due no doubt to the amount of time spent not only designing, but being seen at the right parties and hanging out with the right people.

Nowadays, it's never a designer showing clothes on a catwalk, it is an indulgent designer showing 'off'. The shows are 'mediations' on fashions. None of them really display any liking for women, or the desire to help them look their best. On the contrary, they present them in hideous fashion, which indicates either they have weird misconceptions about women or macabre fantasies.

Despite their claim to be original or innovative the shows follow a pattern. There are usually nerve-jarring string instruments sounding as if they are just tuning up, purporting to be 'mood music'. The setting is either stark, in some warehouse or other, or oddly futuristic with perspective – distorting mirrors; veiled and darkened lights create an atmosphere of gloom. Naturally, the buyers and fashion editors are dazzled into believing the presentation is 'ground breaking'. You must have to do a course in fashion linguistics to attend these shows as they all use the same expressions, delivered with apparent seriousness and fervour.

The models appear and a hush falls over the audience. Walking with measured steps they move into view. Their excessively slow entrance and exit must be due to practicalities as well as 'art'. I doubt they can see where they are going, what with the grim lighting and forest of starched hair and over-painted eyes. The trend for body-piercing must mean that a lot of them are also in pain and any sudden movement would be their downfall.

The clothes are as perplexing as the shows, the price tags beyond belief...

So are the press releases which refer to learned reading and philosophical and cerebral matters. These people regard their work as 'conceptual and aesthetic'; the development is 'constant, obsessive', moving in time with transience of fashion. Goodness knows *where* they get these expressions from; there must be a manual somewhere for the self-consciously avant-garde designer of the 21st Century.

They actually say they *don't* expect people to walk around in their clothes. Usually, the seams are in odd places if they are stitched at all. Or, there are no sleeves and the arms are bound to the body. Maybe the cut of the garment is such that you would be arrested for indecent exposure if you were to wear it in public. So, why do they do it? To get a reaction, to get the fashion writers to say the look is 'minimal in look and maximal in thought".

As a child I loved the story about an Emperor who allowed himself to be deceived by his vanity. His constant quest to be the most splendidly dressed in all his kingdom cost him dearly. Two rogues persuaded him that the invisible cloth they brought to him was the most exquisite in the world. But it could only be seen by intelligent and cultured people. Unwilling to admit they couldn't see the suit as only if they were the brightest and the best. Having been alerted to the visibility concept no one wished to appear a fool, so his subjects cheered the Emperor, discussed the quality and fine workmanship of his clothing.

A young boy ended all this hypocrisy and posturing by declaring (honestly) that the Emperor was not wearing any clothes. The story ends with everyone ending the deception and agreeing that the Emperor was indeed, naked!

An Eye for Detail

Is it my imagination or are manufacturers using smaller print for their instructions? I find the writing on packaging increasingly difficult to decipher, I have also started to have headaches all of which points to the fact that I probably need glasses.

Some people look great in glasses, I don't. I look like a fly. A recent marketing strategy has been to use supermodels to advertise designer frames. Glasses have now become a fashion item.

But old responses die hard and when glasses were simply a response to health. I had a friend who wore glasses. From the time the school nurse sent her home with a note to say she squinted, they played a dominant role in her life. For a start, they were hideous. The National Health Service in England used to provide glasses, but they were nasty steel-rimmed things; circular and owl-like. They made her a figure of fun.

Since my friend's parents could not afford to buy from a private optician, these were what she had to wear. 'Four eyes' she was called at school by our playmates, whether she was wearing them or not. Who says children cannot be cruel?

Most of the time she never had them in her possession; they were always lost, broken or being repaired. She left them on buses, used them as bookmarks, or sat on them sometimes.

The memory of her tears either because she had lost them, or because the frames were broken and repaired with sellotape, is still vivid. She took to hiding them in shame. She went cross-eyed when she looked at anything for more than a second. Everyone thought this was hysterical, so even when she was glasses-free she was the butt of humour.

In the eyes of our small world she was defined as someone who could never look attractive. Actually, she grew up to be the best of the bunch. She bought contact lenses when she started working. With nothing to impede her vision or her confidence, she blossomed into a lovely young woman.

My generation associated glasses with studiousness seriousness or just plain dullness. The youth of today wear them audaciously. Certainly the variety of frames available is greater and more attractive, although the latest expensive trend is to buy designer sunglasses and replace the lens with optic glass. A few years ago my sister almost had to re-mortgage their house to pay for an individualized pair of glasses for my nephew. High fashion means high prices.

But at least this generation makes no apology for wearing glasses. And why should they? They are sensible enough to think seeing clearly *with* glasses is preferable to peering at life though a mist.

By and large my own methods for improving my eyesight have worked. I used to press firmly on the iris which somehow helped my eyes to focus. Lately I use a magnifying glass when practical and when I'm alone.

A lot of people I know wear glasses. They look perfectly nice. Come to think of it, I don't recall many of my female friends and family wearing them. So is it a feminine vanity thing peculiar to our generation? Maybe, I think it also has a lot to do with accepting that we are growing older.

I had an eye-test for my last medical report. I couldn't be sure if my eyes were deceiving me so I said the letters in the order I memorized years ago, just to be on the safe side. The trick obviously worked as no one suggested I needed glasses.

That is unusual these days. Selling glasses is big business. Even pharmacists and small shops sell them in England so there must be a lot of profit to be made. Either eyesight has deteriorated or the general population is growing older.

I suspect it is the latter. Mid-age is a great 'fix-up' time, just as it is in the early years. Teeth need fixing; eyes need fixing and so on. It will probably be painless for the youth of today thirty years on. One zap of a laser will cure all.

It's to be hoped the treatment will also be cheaper. Once people have paid for their children's teeth to be straightened and maintained, provided them with glasses or contact lenses, bought gels, sprays and conditioners for their hair, fed and educated them there's not a lot of money left. When our basically solid structure needs some work we have to dig deep into our pockets.

I suppose it hardly matters to anyone else if I get glasses. But it matters to me and I shall avoid them while I can. All is vanity! When I start to choose books for the size of the print or count myself lucky when I cross the road nearly bumping into a bus, then I will have another eye-test. In the meantime I'm hanging on to my magnifying glass.

Colour Perfect

A friend tried to persuade me to go to a 'Colour Me Beautiful' evening. I need all the help I can get, but I refused to go because I knew the 'expert' would tell me I am an autumn person, or spring or summer. Never, never would she say I am a winter person.

I know all about this stuff. They tell you which season you represent and then dictate which colours you should be wearing. I'd never get away with black and I love it! They say black is not a colour (what is it?) and should be worn with white, only by winter people.

I am not a winter person, I hate the cold and I hate snow. I don't mind looking at it on mountain tops as I fly over in a heated aeroplane. But I don't want to walk in it, ski on it or touch it. You can keep it. However, I do want winter colours I like white, red and black. Strong vibrant colours which make me feel sharp and suave.

My friend says they drain me ... So drain away, let my cheeks fade. Let me have my red coat and my white suit, and my little black dresses ... any style, as long as it's black. I won't let any 'expert' take them away from me.

I'm supposed to wear pink. The last time I wore pink was when I was three years old if you don't include the time I put a red leather glove in the washing machine with my 'whites'. (I don't *know* how I did it). Pink is supposed to be a very calming colour. I wouldn't find it soothing; if I wore pink I'd have a face to match my outfit ... I would feel embarrassed, awkward; shy ... . Maybe it wouldn't come amiss sometimes!

Who are these 'experts' anyhow? Whether they broadcast on the air or on paper we always wonder what their criteria is. How do they select, sort, differentiate and decide what advice to give? What do 'experts' *do* all day? And who made them an 'expert'? You would have to be very confident, possibly egotistical and condescending to be one. Maybe they are born that way, or do they actually train them to tell other people what to do, what to like or dislike, etc.? What a dreary world it would be if we all liked the same things or the same colours come to that.

What about a blue world? Blue is supposed to carry the vibration of trust and reliability. Nice thought. But it would not be welcome somewhere like Iceland as blue, being a cold colour, makes you feel colder. Black would be oppressive I think and brown too boring. What about purple? It often goes with high ideals, loyalty, truth, love and suffering ... It certainly matches the essence of our world. I'd put a few different colour stripes in for variety. But stripes apparently can encourage arguments and confusion; there's enough of that around already.

In the ancient art of Feng Shui, which is all the rage according to interior design experts (there we go again) each colour carries its own vibration. Some colours give energy and warmth, others take it away. Each colour has significance and different colour combinations in different areas of the house affect your health. There must be something in it, why else would the following English expressions have been devised ... feeling blue, in the pink, seeing red, being in a black depression, etc.

I like people with 'colour personalities'. It means they have zest for living, are larger than life, lively and spontaneous. A bit like children really. I love children's paintings with purple cows and tallow skies. When I first started teaching I would try to correct them – now I'm wiser. It's their painting after all, their self-expression. If they want a world of pink seas, red rivers and blue grass, so be it. They know what they like.

I know what I like too. So I will always be a 'before' not an 'after' person. You can't pick up a magazine these days without seeing someone being 'made over'. It's colour coordinating, hair styling, make-up or dieting.

What they do is cut, style and possibly colour someone's hair, then they give them defined lips, 'important' eyes (it's always important) and create cheekbones by darkening just below. After that they put a new outfit which they obviously hate as they look so uncomfortable. Voila! The 'after' person.

The 'before' and 'after' dieter appears without make-up, smile and fetching clothes in before pictures. Afterwards there's a big smile, on a fully made-up face with tailored clothes and classy shoes. No wonder they look better.

What always crosses my mind is that when you've removed all the finery and the make-up goes down the drain the party's over. What you see is what you are.

A New Image

I had to move everything out of my wardrobe recently as the bedroom ceiling needed repairing. It took almost three hours to lift everything out and re-hang it elsewhere. The amount of clothing I have stashed away came as a shock. When I buy something new I just push everything along to create some space. Thus I have enough clothes to dress the inhabitants of a small town.

It made me feel guilty because a lot of the stuff hasn't seen the light of day for a very long time. My husband commented on the fact that he had never seen me wear a lot of the items. That's partly because the wardrobe is so tightly packed, it's an effort to find anything. I'd taken to opening it just a crack and rotating five or six items.

It has become awesome in scale, hiding so many impulse buys, endless pairs of shoes and 'forgotten' dresses with the price tag still hanging. I didn't need them and I obviously don't even *want* them!

I was recently taken upstairs to look at the staggering shoe collection belonging to my friend's husband. I didn't say a lot. She seemed to think he had far too many shoes. They were a drop in the ocean compared to my collection! Half of it has gone out of fashion, some of the shoes pinch or are unsuitable for my lifestyle. He doesn't need all those shoes, he doesn't even like a lot of them, but it never occurs to me to throw them out. It would be a waste of money, wouldn't it?

My husband says this is applying my personal (and peculiar) logic. The money was wasted in the first place, buying things I didn't need.

I like clothes, but I often envy the simplicity of his wardrobe. He's never at a loss to know what to wear, nor does he take forever to find it, because there's not that much choice. My impulse is to throw everything of mine out, and to start again simply. But even I can see that would not be a reasonable thing to do.

I need one of those 'make-over' experts, an image consultant. These people revamp women's wardrobes. The object is to edit your wardrobe. The first things to go are 'some day' clothes; 'some day when I go somewhere really special I'll wear this', and 'some day when we vacation in Hawaii I'll wear this', or 'some day I'll get this altered to fit and I'll wear it'.

I've got an enormous collection of smart winter clothes in Jeddah because 'some day' we'll go on holiday from Jeddah to somewhere cold. Then I'll really need them, won't I? The problem is cold climates don't attract us. The only place we go where it is sometimes cold is England, and I don't pack winter clothes as I have plenty to go home to. Meanwhile, my 'some day' clothes are probably going out of fashion. I have alteration plans, but I never find the time to even remove the clothes from their polythene covers.

A lot of women have a wardrobe containing enough material for a psychologist's seminar. Its contents are like a record of past holidays and past lives. There are so many options to deal with when you are trying to find the 'right' outfit to go out. My husband and daughter bear witness to many occasions when I've tried on such a variety of clothes that I am worn out by the time I'm feeling I have made the right choice and I am ready to go out.

Women don't really dress to please themselves or even their husbands. Place, purpose, formality, and especially the hostess, have to be considered. And I have friends with teenagers who refuse to go out with their parents if mum insists on looking 'like that'.

A lot of us have wonderful clothes which we don't wear for practical reasons it will crease during the car journey, the baby might be sick down it or we might spill something on it. Yet clothes are for wearing so there really is no point in owning something if you never put it on. There are plenty of other reasons why we don't wear them... We don't look good in them or they are outdated. But we hang on to them because they cost a fortune, and perhaps the biggest reason is because we have too many of them.

There I've said it! I have too many clothes and I hoard them. If I changed on the hour for the rest of my life, I still wouldn't be able to get through them all.

I should get rid of my old favourites. I've got things that don't look tired but I don't wear them because I've got those easy-to-wear favourites. I actually sorted them out once but they somehow crept out of the bin-liner.

Where's my will-power? I think I lost it in the changing-rooms of countless shops. Fashion editors have the knack of making you believe you can't live without the season's 'look'. The trouble is the season is short-lived and you're left with all those fashionable-for-five minutes things.

That ceiling-repair could prove to be *very* expensive. When I've the time and the determination, I am going to hire an image consultant!

Retail Therapy

I used to have a silver disc attached to my key-ring with 'Born to Shop' engraved on it. Over the years it wore thin, along with my interest in shopping sprees. Women are often accused of being shopaholics, coming home with bags of new clothes and over-used credit cards. I was that woman!

Now, just the thought of browsing around the shops is liable to make me break into a cold sweat. I find it boring and a waste of time. The only thing worse than actual shopping is 'window shopping.' Imagine using time and energy looking at things you don't want or can't afford. If people want to look at beautiful things, they would be better off in an art gallery.

I didn't always feel like this: I used to spend a lot of time in shops trying on clothes and shoes or testing make-up. I bought a lot of things I didn't need, and even things I didn't really want. It was a form of escapism I don't need now.

According to a recent survey, one in five adults classed themselves as reluctant shoppers. Perhaps everyone has found something more interesting to do and is unwilling to devote so much of their free time to shopping. More likely, people are finding themselves squeezed for time from every direction. We can't linger round the shops anymore. This is probably why shops that sell, everything are so popular, you can buy everything you need in one go ... So we all fall prey to the Mega-Stores which steadily increase their prices in the certain knowledge we haven't time to revert to shopping around, taking note of prices and going to different shops for the best bargains.

The issue of Supermarkets over-charging is of increasing concern. Retailers are in the business of satisfying their shareholders nowadays. The days of consumer-power are over. We are in the hands of Supermarkets, who are abusing their dominance and we cannot escape – because we haven't time to!

So, with little time on our hands shopping is no longer therapeutic. It has become a necessary evil. The shops are too crowded and there is too much choice, so many a decision becomes impossible. To buy a pair of socks, for example, you have to decide if you would like plain or patterned, wool, cotton, with lycra, without lycra, long or short ... it's enough to make you run around bare-foot!

The choices, the crowds and the certain knowledge that I already have too much of everything makes me reject 'retail therapy'. I want to stay away from the shops; if I go, I know I will buy. I will be lured by the soft-sell of sweet music, attractive decor and kaleidoscope of colour into buying something I don't need, or even really want.

Mail order has enjoyed increasing popularity among like-minded people, and it seems there are many. Mail order is big business and people are enjoying making choices in the comfort of their own homes without even one 'pushy' salesperson giving unrequited advice. When the goods arrive you can try them out, or try them on, at leisure, and if you are not satisfied the firm will exchange or refund, without making you feel you've committed a crime. When I return unsatisfactory clothing or footwear to a retail shop I am always 'the only customer who has complained', and no wonder when the sales staff turn it into a major issue. You have to be strong and determined to win the 'battle'. And when you do, you feel you have to slink out of the place with every eye boring into your back. This is probably why so many women have unworn clothes tucked away somewhere; keeping them is easier.

We'll soon be able to save time and shoe leather. The home shopping market is forecast to grow by tens of billions by the beginning of the next century.

The Internet is one of the biggest growth areas offering more potential to those who don't want to leave home to fill their shopping bags. The website is so convenient. Just sit in front of the computer and log on to the required retailer. Like in a mail order catalogue, there are pictures to help you make your decision. The computer pops everything into you basket and when you've finished you click on your size, type in your credit card number and it's done. The computer even gives you a receipt and the goods are delivered a few days later.

You can buy most of your presents on the Internet too and you don't have to spend hours wrapping gifts and writing cards. There are new Companies and shops going on-line every day.

It won't *all* be 'retail therapy', there is always a price to pay for progress and the cost will not only be attached to the goods. But the thought of Supermarket shopping on the Internet with my virtual trolley, is very attractive. You avoid queuing and having to carry heavy bags home. I won't begrudge paying other people to do the hard work at all! I can't wait!

Scent of Success

A few years ago, my teenage nephew asked for a designer fragrance. I was somewhat taken aback, this request coming from a youth who wouldn't even eat fruit, because it was, he said, 'girlie food'. Also, I had become accustomed to Englishmen either wearing an aromatic after-shave or an overpowering deodorant, if anything at all. Mostly they smelled of soap sweat or sometimes tobacco.

Centuries ago, before the advent of bathrooms and a daily washing ritual, the upper classes doused themselves with heavy, intense perfumes to disguise the smell of their body odours. This was during the period when people, in general, were washed twice in their lives, at birth and at death. It was long ago and since people began bathing regularly perfumes have been used as a personal adornment for the fairer sex.

Times are changing and European men are no longer afraid to define their identity by the fragrance they wear. There are fragrances to suit every personality be they suave and sophisticated, sporty, intellectual or adventurous. The trend may have been initiated by men, but it has certainly been perpetuated by clever marketing.

At first the Perfume Houses around the World, who traditionally created perfumes for women, began to make versions of the same for men; But the new creations, whose singular names evoke character, masculinity, energy and power, target men of any generation with natural fragrances which are modern and classically elegant.

The new perfumes have to match the mood of the Times both in terms of presentation and the smell. Even if the perfume is sensational it won't sell unless the bottle, packaging and marketing is equally effective. People are being sold a dream nowadays and that dream changes in accordance with our way of life and values. The Designers must anticipate these changes; they have to know what we want before we do! What comes first the chicken of the egg? I don't know. We seem to be a society of people seduced and cajoled by advertising magnets.

Whatever your view, you have to pay homage to these creative people who predict future trends. Some have achieved celebrity status. A quiet American has become internationally recognizable by his initials. He is an amazing designer whose clothes and fragrances have become synonymous with youth, style simplicity and sophistication. He has transcended class, sex and age barriers. I want his clothes and fragrances and so do the very young. Parents with children as young as ten years find his creations on the list of 'must haves'.

Youth and women enslaved he has moved on to capture the male market but produces the kind of scents we women, like to steal from our men. I saw today he has launched yet another highly original fragrance; he moves on, we move on...

So do the times in which we live and people seem to want a kind of therapy in the fragrance they choose ... Something to make you feel good as advanced technology takes over our lives and there is less altruism and more individualism (selfishness). So we seek the comfort and nostalgia of our roots when life felt safe.

Ozonic and food notes are being included, giving an original twist to their universal appeal. Our favourite smell, be it fresh fruits, newly mown hay, vanilla, chocolate or a newborn baby's skin are the undertones of many new perfumes.

Certain fragrances linger in the memory. The idealised memory of the scents of Saudi Arabia I will carry with me always. Whenever I smell the sweet, rich aroma of dates or the sharp, fruity smell of oranges, I will think of Saudi ... Desert musk, the spicy tones of cardamom, coriander, ginger and the intense charm of jasmine, camellia and sandalwood are exotic and captivating I will remember the coffee shop's stimulating aroma, the hotel lobbies' classically elegant scent, the focus on simplicity and well being; the upmarket shops' pervading fragrance; opulent, rich; perfumed oils in every shopping mall enticing, intense, with elegant glass bottles to please the eye. The smell of the fruit tobaccos used in the shishe, the smoking, heady incense burners. A melon sweet and ripe, flowers in blossom, rose water, the tantalizing aroma of roasting meat, newly pulled mint, these too will ever remind me of Saudi Arabia.

Bad Hair Day

I watched my sister's neighbour going off to a wedding. She must have had to re-mortgage the house to pay for the suit she was wearing and her hat was spectacular. The morning had been spent at a beauty salon; with her new hairstyle and artful make-up, she looked and felt radiant.

The next day I asked "How was the wedding?" I knew how much she had been looking forward to the occasion and was very surprised when she said she'd had an awful time. Apparently, when she took off her hat at the Reception Party, her hair was a disaster. Under the hat, it had flattened on top and bent at odd angles under the stylish rim. She convinced herself that her horrible hair was the only thing people noticed about her. She'd be remembered as 'the woman with the freakish hair'. It had spoiled everything.

It sounds trivial perhaps, but if a woman's hair is a mess it dominates her thoughts and affects her mood. Women see their hair as an extension of themselves, so if it is not looking good they feel awful.

Most women can give a long biography of their hair. We have a complex relationship with what grows out of our heads. Sometimes we nurture it, it supports us and we feel great. At other times we play around with it – chopping it off, colouring it, curling or straightening it. One thing's for certain; every woman born with curly hair will do anything and everything to get it straight, whilst women blessed with straight hair will often perform all manner of techniques to get it to curl.

I had glorious curls when I was a baby; as it grew it became straight. I didn't really notice it until I was about five or six years old. I remember catching sight of myself in my Mother's dressing-table mirror and thinking my fringe was too long. Using a pair of nail scissors I attended to it. I was quite pleased with the effect until I heard my Mother scream. Bizarre haircuts were not in vogue in those days.

My punishment was to live in that state until it grew back which took a long time. There we have the main trouble with my hair ... Just when I got it where I wanted it, I'd go and do something stupid and then the only way to save it was to have it all cut off. Many disastrous attempts to have permanently curly hair have ended up on the floor at the hairdressers.

The painful cycle of growing is long and irritating. I marvel at music and film stars today. One minute they appear bald, the next they have long luscious curls.

Growing hair is a preoccupation with little girls. Unless they have tomboy instincts, all little girls want long hair. When it is nothing more than fluffy down, it is an anguished wait. The world seems full of long-haired people. Even dogs have more hair than you do.

I grew mine very long and I delighted in its arrow-straight quality for many years. Then the fashion changed and I cut it off to my shoulders, where it obediently curled under. But then I thought it looked boring, so what did I do, I curled it. I didn't look trendy so I had a boyish cut, but with it spiked at the top. I imagined I could 'wash and go' but it took a vast number of products and a lot of work with a tail comb to keep it in shape. I had it cut even shorter and this time I did cry every time I saw myself in a mirror. I avoided looking but would sometimes catch sight of my crew cut in shop windows. I used to wet it a lot – because wet hair looks longer. Even that miserable interlude didn't teach me a lesson I kept making changes ... and mistakes.

According to social psychologists hair can speak volumes about us. We use it to make statements about ourselves, just as we do our clothes. And when I look back into the history of my hair it does reflect the moods and relationships I was in. I haven't done anything extreme to my hair for a few years. Now something momentous has happened in my life and I find myself thinking of a change. However, I haven't got the time, right now, to cope with anything else that is new – but that is the only thing stopping me!

The state of your hair can make the difference between feeling that you could take on the world or wanting to hide at home. Although it wasn't the case in earlier times, men for some considerable time simply cut their hair when it grew too long and washed it when it was dirty.

Then they started to grow it in the 1960's and you were hard-pressed to guess whether you were looking at a male or a female from behind. Later it was tamed into pony-tails. Even middle-aged men (who should have known better) grew their thinning locks and scraped all they had into a sorry tail at the back of their heads.

Then came the razor cuts ... underneath at strange angles across partings or creating amazing patterns on the scalp until finally the lot was shaved off. Futuristic '21st century Men' appeared in the high streets much to the chagrin of men unhappy to be bald by fate of nature.

One World Cup saw the advent of coloured hair for more flamboyant players. Some of these football players are role models and while I've yet to see green hair off the pitch, there are dozens of David Beckham look-alikes.

Equal opportunity works both ways and we must be prepared to share our hair products with our husbands if not already doing so. And we'll both have bad hair days though hopefully, not on the same day!

Trying Too Hard

The nature of happiness is fast becoming a hot topic among social scientists. Their research is linking this emotion to a whole range of different factors and influences. Linked with wealth or simplicity, freedom or commitment, happiness is dangled in front of us in countless advertisements. So how do we get it, can it be bought, must it be carned?

One study shows that laughter can boost your happiness level; another shows that time alone each day makes people more sociable, productive and happy. But what most experts seem to agree is that the true source of happiness lies within you, rather than on external forces. So whether you are rich or poor, there is no significant difference in happiness levels – provided, of course, you are not so poor that you have nothing to eat and nowhere to live!

Like everything else worth having, happiness cannot be handed to you on a plate. We can be happy experiencing the passive pleasure of warm sunshine, a delicious meal or a well-rested body. But this kind of happiness is dependent on favourable circumstances. The happiness we create ourselves grows within. It is of our own making and rarely occurs while we are involved in purely passive activities, such as watching television. If we approached life more actively we'd probably feel happier. The problem is you have to sum up the initial effort required before activities become enjoyable.

While we all need to relax and 'chill-out' once in a while, we'd feel much better if we devoted as much attention to our free time as we do to our jobs. The amount of satisfaction we derive from even the most routine jobs is proportional to the amount of effort we put into them.

Perhaps it's even more important to develop the habit of doing things with concentrated attentiveness. Children do that and children are generally happy. It doesn't mean being constantly active; children are frequently contemplative and happiness can come from thought as well as action.

I've read a lot recently about the pursuit of happiness It appeared to be the 'must-have' for the new millennium. Politicians, film stars and the like now follow 'happiness gurus'; believe it or not. These people are paying over the odds to learn that happiness is found in a state of mind, in complete immersion in whatever you're involved with – from playing sport to talking to friends. Has 21st Century Man lost touch with reality to such an extent we have to re-learn that?

Therapies, happiness gurus and even consultants who offer to help you make a happiness plan – you make a life plan instead of the one backward looking 'Where did I go wrong?' type of assessment. Later you introduce the concept of quality control which is basically a matter of nipping any dissatisfaction in the bud.

Is all this *really* necessary though? Whatever happiness is, it is surely just a part of life. Perhaps it is meant to be elusive. Maybe it is wrong to spend so much time in pursuit of happiness. The Chinese believe you will never find happiness until you stop looking for it. I don't think that is necessarily true, but there are times when our expectations are too high. We cannot expect to feel happy all of the time. We all feel down now and then. Feeling like this is normal and we usually manage to bounce back again without needing to rush off to the doctor. This is not depression – it's simply a time when life's not as enjoyable as it can be.

Depression is feeling sad for a long time and when people may feel loss of hope for the future. Many people believe themselves to be suffering from depression when in reality their low spirits are quite normal. These days however, we are led to believe if we are not feeling happy all the time then there is something wrong with us. We've grown so spoilt and selfish that we demand happiness as one of our rights, or at the very least, expect to be able to buy it.

My Grandmother was a cheerful person who laughed and sang a lot as she worked at her household tasks. If I'd asked her if she was happy, she would have told me she was too busy to think about it. But she was happy I think. She tackled every task no matter how mundane or routine with such vigour that it brought her satisfaction and pride in a job well done.

If we changed the way we look at life we would be happier and more relaxed. Children never see holidays in terms of airport hassles or packing problems. A heavy downpour is a thrill; it's rushing out into the rain and splashing in puddles, not concern about road conditions and getting your clothes wet.

For young children the world is full of new discoveries. The sense of wonder and the ability to be amazed is something we lose as we grow older. We start to take all those day to day experiences for granted and in doing so miss out a lot of simple pleasures. In the words of a famous English novelist, George Orwell, 'Men can only be happy when they do not assume that the object of life is happiness'.

A Price To Pay

I have a friend in her thirties who has recently been promoted. Not only does she have her own criteria for the day because it is a management position, she has also to deal with other people's problems and mistakes. She has to keep everything running smoothly and does so very competently. A home and children, a husband and an active social life are also on her agenda. Always well-groomed, pleasant and calm, she appears to be coping extremely well. But, because I am her friend, I know she has a price to pay in terms of personal well-being and health.

Working too hard and for too many hours, she has delegated the care of her home and her children to someone she pays. Whilst this help is essential there are times when she is aware she is, in her words, "not a good mother". In traditional terms, she is not; she will have missed out on those few and precious years when your children truly depend on you. Before they discover independence, their own interests and set of friends, they want to be the centre of your world, the focus of all your attention.

My friend knows all this, but she wants to give them all the things she never had, she says. More than that she wants to remain 'herself', to stay financially and personally independent.

There is a whole new generation who feel the same as they did in their twenties but now have a mortgage and children. They are the generation of 'late youth'. They are privileged and self-centred, double-salaried, with grand homes and two or more cars. Certain areas in the countries in which they live become fashionable and this group tend to live side by side. They live among like-minded people. People who are in control of their finances and their lives. They are choosing to have fewer children, or not to have children at all.

Healthier diets, improved lifestyles and a wide-spread desire to feel younger for longer has changed the status quo. There was a time when thirty-plus meant middle-age. Now people live longer and have a totally new set of values.

Money has a lot to do with it and education. People have money in their pockets and what they are buying is independence.

The work factor means that men and women work hard and play hard. There is potential for the realisation of their dreams and ambitions.

This largely selfish group display a new trend to be both parent and child. They are not trying to recapture their youth, they have never lost it. Mothers and fathers compete with their children in clothing, social engagements and attention. They use each other's first names, 'Mum' and 'Dad' seeming outmoded.

They are a generationally blinkered group. There were once clear cut guidelines to what should be achieved at different ages. The real substance of maturity is lost now; the contented realisation that you have achieved so much and are comfortable with yourself. With the current potential for time-stretching, people look younger and are healthier. Financial concerns pose no threat, they have help in the home and someone to look after the children.

Running alongside the obvious benefits these people enjoy are enormous pressures... to maintain their lifestyle, to look young, to keep their jobs from younger, competitive newcomers, to stay 'on top'.

Stress is our reaction to the pressures we face. Whilst stress can 'give you the edge', keeps the adrenaline flowing and can make people perform well, it also has a detrimental effect. There are mental and physical manifestations of this. People can become nervy, depressed, volatile or bad tempered. It takes its toll on health too. Although my friend appears to deal with her stress, she is concerned that her skin is becoming dry and spotty, that her nails keep splitting and her hair comes out in handfuls. These are some of the signs of stress and she will have to deal with them.

Dealing with stress has become big business. Many firms employ stress-managers, masseurs, exercise teachers or meditation techniques. They are also looking to the Far East for ancient remedies, from furniture reorganisation, to colour schemes and food to create a feeling of well-being for their employees. This is not totally altruistic. Stress is the cause of the majority of illnesses and absenteeism from work these days.

'The higher you climb, the farther you fall' is an old maxim in my country. Whilst it is marvellous to be offered so much in terms of opportunity, materialism and personal freedom, there is a heavy penalty to pay, which may be too great for some.

Dressed for Success

I guess I wasn't the only one groping about their wardrobe for something to wear for work. I don't exactly slob about on holiday, but my choice of clothing is, let's say, more relaxed. Now it's back to work and my options are not wide open. Firstly, I need to be prepared for at least one of the children in my class to paint my outfit, or to glue it to the table. So 'designer labels' are out. So are the clothes which I like the best, the ones which suit me best and the ones my husband bought for me.

A workman's boiler-suit though ideal, would not be tolerated. Trousers would be practical, but none of mine fit the description of acceptable leg-wear. So skirts and dresses it is. These must be wide enough for ease of movement but not voluminous, lest you lose an infant in the folds.

I wish they would devise a school uniform for teachers. You would never have to worry *what* to wear nor feel anyone's clothes were smarter than yours. We actually designed one in a school in which I was working in Germany. But the school governors wouldn't let us wear red, so the idea was dropped.

I watched a remarkable hour of television in the holidays, about dressing for work. It featured career women in New York. They take their appearance very seriously. It is a priority, they say and they work really hard at it. Looking good is part of being successful for them.

These businesswomen are capable, but working hard is not enough when it comes to attaining career success in such a competitive city. First impressions are important; that want to promote the image of a dynamic woman who knows exactly where she's going.

It is a designer culture; they dedicate time to shopping and looking good. There are beauty salons and manicure parlours on every corner of the city. We even watched a business meeting taking place in a nail parlour where the two managers were having a pedicure. Gross!

They all have a make-up lady and a personal hairdresser to do a 'touch up' half way through the day. And the day starts early, before 6:00 a.m. with a strict exercise programme to keep in shape. Personal trainers are common place.

"I want it all", said one woman, "I want a flat stomach, the best clothes, neat hair and good looks. I want to have the edge over everybody else."

The woman portrayed in the documentary had learned to put their assertiveness on display. Lack of self-confidence could lead to the spoiling of promotion prospects. It's a tough world out there, in American business, and these women are sharp.

It's not just the employees realising the value of assertiveness, but employers as well. Many companies are learning that having confident and capable staff is in their interest too. They are rushing to provide courses on personal development and assertiveness together with seminars on power-dressing. They employ make-up artists, hairdressers and fashion experts to advise their staff, knowing the image they project reflects on the Company.

The TV programme alone exhausted me let alone the practicalities. So how do they do it? Are these Superwomen? When do they find time to be with their families, see friends, reflect on what they are doing or relax?

What the programme failed to show and what is most likely is a full 'support team' in the background. This will consist in part of family and friends but also a lot of hired help; people to do the housework, laundry and to look after their kids. I've got friends like them. This is how they manage their domestic arrangements and their lives do not resemble those of ordinary women at all. They feel the need for better childcare facilities and for support in recognising the family in all forms. Husbands take on their share of childcare; some men even give up their jobs to stay at home, which is no bad thing.

I'm not about to start a debate on working mothers. Women are financially and personally driven to work outside the home. It was an article in last Tuesday's paper that started me thinking about it. The article from San Francisco, reported a research set to examine whether youth of today – dubbed 'Generation X' is really more world weary and unhappy than previous generations. The results indicated that current discontent and cynicism is experienced by everyone; youth is not alone. It makes you think…

"Excuse Me, There's a Fly in My Soup"

Traditionally English people don't complain, at least not in public. They maintain the British stiff upper-lip; we're renowned for it. All over the world restaurants can get away with indifferent service and unappetizing food, served at inflated prices with inpecunity. Few people will object. I once took a summer job in a small English restaurant by the sea. Trade was seasonal and the majority of customers were day visitors. The food served was inferior to the meals my Mother gave her dog; in fact she wouldn't have given it to her dog. But people would pay their bills and leave behind plates of barely touched food and not one person ever complained. The amount we threw away demonstrated how little they liked it, but no one said a word. The owners were acquitted of a bad reputation because there were always newcomers to serve I used to make certain I never caught anyone's eye as I shamefully put the food in front of them ... But, as Roosevelt is reported to have said "You can't be anyone's victim without giving your permission."

But times are changing; slowly but surely. In the same way we have followed the Americans in many aspects of life, so their inclination to sue at the drop of a hat is catching on. Lawyers are now permitted to advertise. Given the bills they present, one would imagine they are already among the wealthiest in the land. However, it appears they need business. Advertisements appear in English newspapers inviting people who have suffered physical or mental anguish to contact the law firm to seek financial recompense. And people are coming forward to make themselves heard.

The Americans have almost turned it into an art form. It's become part of their culture to believe that no matter what happens to you someone else is responsible. Most notable in recent years were the cases against Tobacco Companies. The plaintiffs had virtually smoked themselves to death and reacted by suing the Cigarette manufactures; people in France and England, to date, have followed suit. The fact that these smokers put the cigarettes to their own lips and puffed smoke into their lungs for decades appears to be someone else's fault. Odd!

Regarding everyday provocation, Latinos are volatile and voluble both in word and gesture when expressing their satisfaction. Teutonic races are stern and uncompromising when they remonstrate at inferior standards. People in Jeddah are very clear about what they regard as good service and quality. Whilst very direct in their criticism they remain cool whilst complaining. We pay for what we get; we have the right to demand value.

So why do the British baulk at finding fault? They don't make known their grievance, verbalize their annoyance, shout or moan, until the bottled-up frustrations spurt like venom from a snake. It tends to be something minor that is the catalyst, the 'straw that breaks the camel's back'. Then, stand back, a life time of complacency bites the dust someone is seriously angry!

Young people are good at it, they complain about everything. They are quick to criticize, uncompromising in their demands. It may be time that curtails indignation, annihilates expectations. Or it could be our increasing preoccupation with the weather!

Dampened Spirits

Cool this morning, after the rain. The bushes drip, the bougainvillea droops; everything has been disturbed, surprised by the deluge. A cock crows incessantly, a thin weedy call. I picture a scraggy, worn bird of pathos. It is disoriented, for the dawn is an hour away.

I navigate gigantic puddles, splash through streams of running water. The water collects everywhere, at every corner, every incline. It's slippery; battered leaves soaked and sodden underfoot. I tread with care; my footsteps resound on the wet roads.

Around the corner I am confronted by a desert dog. Shocked, I stop dead. We stare at each other ... I walk away, glancing nervously over my shoulder. It dips back into the shadows. It may have been driven into the compound by the rain, or hunger; there are rich pickings in our bins.

Adrenaline courses through my veins I feel weak with fright. I make my way to the far side of the compound and continue my run, still shaking. I focus my attention on my bruised toenail. The top of my trainer rests squarely on it. It hurts, distracts me from my fear.

Lightning flashed over the water of the creek brightens the darkness; I forget the dog, find a rhythm in my pace and start to think...

Someone owes me money. This dominates my thoughts today. It's not simply a question of money; it's an ugly situation, irritating and embarrassing. I feel I can't ask for it again. It makes me feel awkward. Besides, they are playing games with me ... silly, avoidance tactics. I would leave them be if I didn't see them spending money freely, some of it mine probably!

I didn't want to lend it in the first place. I've been in this position before by not refusing similar requests. My problem is, I can't say 'no'. I'm shouting it inside my head. When to agree doesn't seem right, but I cannot force that tiny word from my lips!

I like to help people when I can. However, my good nature is sometimes abused. I once went on an 'assertiveness course', to learn I have the right to say no. You can still be a good person and refuse to do things now and then. The Course leaders warned us not to become victims of our eagerness to please. Well, I stayed assertive for the entire course, stunning friends and family by my refusals. Eventually, I went back to my old ways, what is natural to me. It feels right.

The disadvantage is that it sometimes creates problems. I'm concerned now by my lack of courage. I've lost more than money. Once trust and respect has gone so has friendship. I don't trust them anymore and they obviously, have no respect for me.

I should have been more circumspect. The reason given for approaching me for a loan ought to have made me wary ... It was simply because I am (quote) 'a nice person'.

I hate the word 'nice'. At face value it is short, easily spelt and a useful adjective if you cannot be more effusive. It is certainly over-used and too much of anything is nauseating. It can mean pleasant or agreeable, desirable qualities surely. But it has begun to carry slightly derogatory undertones. Being described as satisfactory seems rather disparaging, as if one is weak, a 'push over' perhaps.

We tend to describe people as 'nice' if we can't find anything special to say about them. It conveys an image of someone near, inoffensive and quite unremarkable in any way!

I don't want to be thought of as 'a nice person'. It's odd how many words have taken on a different meaning from their origin; depending on the context in which they are used, and current fads. I have a strong will and I'm sometimes very disagreeable. So don't call me nice ... and don't try to borrow money from me!

England's Promise

William Wordsworth was an English poet who was born and lived most of his life in the Lake District, which is one of the most picturesque areas of England. His major theme was the relationship between man and nature. As school-children we knew him as an interminably long winded poet. Add to this, the compulsory memorizing of 'I wandered lonely as a cloud', and the result was we didn't like him very much.

I like poetry and now I am older I am more susceptible to his work. And I have to admit that all through my life I have remembered the words of the poem we were forced to learn. Actually, committing it to memory wasn't the problem. The difficulty lay in having to recite it in front of the whole class and the teacher, ever ready to pounce if you made a mistake.

The poem describes 'a host of golden daffodils', English flowers, which are bright as the sun and herald the end of winter they are much loved because they are beautiful and especially because they mark the turning of the seasons.

Spring comes and there is warmth again, new growth, new hopes and dreams.

During an extended holiday I saw winter turn to spring over a few days. Walking along the road it felt warmer; although the wind was so strong I had to battle against it. By the side of the grim paths, monotonously grey, yellow daffodils swayed and danced. Then I noticed the paths were dappled with sunlight, and yet more spring flowers had emerged in all their glory. Buds on the trees had started to show, with the promise of green soon to come. It is an almost indescribable feeling, that 'lifting of the heart', when you realize the dark and cold of winter is over.

There was a nip in the air; the frosty air pinched, reddening checks and noses, biting fingers and toes. But the promise of spring put a smile on people's faces and they called 'Good Morning'. It was a good morning, a great start to the day.

I love the changes of season, the sharp contrasts in climate and scenery. And England remains stubbornly divided socially even though the country has formed a political whole. The jigsaw-parts have resolutely retained their character.

England is a most intricate jigsaw, with each of its parts different from the next. Although it is relatively small it is too varied a country for any one person to get to know in a lifetime.

The land is cliffs and mountains, lanes and city streets, fields and beaches, farms and industrial landscapes. There are rivers, streams and lakes and the inescapable sea which encircles the island. Each region has varied geological features, different types of people the way of life, even the food changes from county to county.

We speak of the North/South divide; unofficial unwritten elitism. Northerners tend to be larger, more expansive and louder than people from the South. Southerners are cooler, more aloof and reserved. Their clothes are more tailored, their food refined with a taste for International cuisine. Northerners eat hearty traditional meals, eye-popping portions rise high on the plates.

I don't see how the European Community can really mean much to the average Briton. The seas that surround the country may be less of a frontier than they were, but they still reinforce our belief that we are a particular type of people and that there are differences among nations. Of course there are and the World's a fascinating place because of it. England's charm also lies in its diversity.

Some people never see it. Despite the fact that travel is easy and the country small, some English people have never seen Scotland, Ireland and Wales nor even visited the capital city London.

Towns and villages everywhere are alarmed by threats of intrusion into their traditional ways of life. The wooden fence, or a hedgerow, is a British symbol of privacy, which is almost defensive. The Englishman's home is bounded this way, his plot of land, however small, separate from the rest. The barriers may be invisible between villages, towns or counties but each is separate. There is a divide which is given mutual respect. Even accents change with the locality, coupled with peculiar local vocabulary, leads to mutual incomprehensibility.

The weather is a major topic of conversation. People comment on the day's climate and speculate on the weather to come. Television and radio forecasts are frequent and detailed. The changes in the weather are a guiding light. No one ventures out of doors without knowing what the weather is going to be like. You can have rain, strong winds, sunshine and even snow on the same day.

It is very likely the United Kingdom will change; we're going through an evolution which many call 'the national decline'. Identity is the question of the times, and the search for identity within Europe is bewildering and complex. This is partly because no one is sure we want to be part of Europe or part of anything but the British Isles. We have been led into it by our politicians, who appear to be dancing to a different tune to the majority of ordinary people.

They will not lead us there like lambs to the slaughter. There's a whirling mass of contradiction in the British psyche for the European Community to deal with. The British are stubborn and the unbounded freedom to live life as one wishes has produced eccentricity and confidence.

Nor do we forget that during two world wars courageous people and soldiers from every walk of life showed they were willing to die for this country of ours.

There are some places in the World which remind one of the landscape of England ... but there is nowhere quite like it!

Can You Take It?

Compliments and criticism ... The chances are you will encounter one or the other today. Both have a powerful effect on our mood and behaviour. It's hard to say which has the stronger effect. Criticism is a negative force and it need not be overt, implied criticism is enough to weaken the resolve of the strongest individual. A person who has been criticized suffers a loss of confidence and that affects the way they behave.

A critical boss does not bring out the best in his employees. Whether they deserved it, or not, it does not serve as a motivator. It takes time for them to 'lick their wounds', to regain equilibrium, and sum up enough confidence to get on with the job. Criticism is generally an ineffective means of improving a situation. It is cruel and makes people fearful and timid. The ploy is of weakness not strength.

Most people respond to praise and encouragement. A clever employer can make someone work harder, more efficiently and cheerfully with a well-timed compliment. My husband told me he learned early on in business to criticize collectively and to compliment them individually. Clever stuff! Everyone feels good about themselves and when things go wrong they share the blame and work together to put things right.

I hadn't thought of it before, but that's exactly what I do in a classroom. The children share the responsibility for putting things right and no individual suffers alone, bearing the weight of the teacher's wrath!

Many positive things are unsaid because of self-consciousness. It's a great pity as a compliment can make someone happy all day.

Compliments are essential in social well-being. We all know how great we feel when someone says we look nice, or we are doing a good job. It's easy to discern whether or not it's sincere. You can tell from someone's voice or expression whether they mean what they are saying.

Sales assistants employ this tactic to induce people to make purchases they are unsure about. They tell Madam (or Sir) that 'blue is your colour', or something equally trite. It is deceitful and I hate it. It is an insincere form of flattery. Sadly, there are lots of people who respond to this ploy, either because they lack self confidence, or they want to believe it's true.

Some people tend to 'fish for compliments'. We all know someone who can't receive enough compliments. Admire their suit and they will ask if you like their shoes ... Eating at their home and saying "This fish is delicious" won't suffice. They'll say "Is the sauce alright? I was worried it wouldn't work ..."

Or else they will compliment you in an extravagant way so you will praise them. This shows a serious lack of self-esteem that no amount of flattery will fix.

Nothing is more flattering than feeling someone has noticed something special about you. That is why being specific, rather than a generalized comment like, "You look nice", is much better.

Compliments are a sign of affection, of an acknowledged closeness between you. There is a sliding scale, depending on how close you are. If you don't know someone well, a comment about the way they look is appropriate. But as your relationship deepens it's good to compliment the non-visual, broader aspects of their personality. Being told "You're so generous'" is a good feeling.

You have to do a mental re-check before paying a compliment sometimes, "you look like you've lost weight" implies they were fat before. And it's better to say "That new hair-style suits you" rather than "you look fantastic. What have you done to yourself?" The latter is a very back-handed compliment, and could easily give offense.

One needs to learn how to accept a compliment gracefully. When you are young, you tend to be very shy and mutter "What this old thing! You like this? I think it makes me look fat". It's best to be grateful and give a brief. "Thank you".

I remember reading that British women should learn to accept a compliment like a French woman. No matter how fulsome the praise Madam would merely smile graciously and murmur "Merci". The problem with the British is that they think that merely accepting a compliment proves we are offensively pleased with ourselves.

It is silly because you can instigate a 'fight'. Disagreeing with the person paying the compliment is actually quite rude; you are questioning their judgment. The other person may feel crushed and wish they hadn't bothered.

It's also a mistake to get into 'competitive complimenting'. One compliment doesn't deserve another. I was once praised by a friend and so I looked her up and down for an outstanding feature only to come out with "Your shoes look really shiny". If you want to say something nice when a friend says you look good, it's best to make a genuine – sounding "So do you" suffice!

Changing Times

I want to buy a greetings card for my brother. It sounds a simple enough task. There are thousands of shops which sell cards and so many companies which produce them. It must be a lucrative business. Increasing numbers of people are sending cards on many different occasions. The cost is also increasing; they are expensive now. But the manufacturers may have to adjust their price policy since computer-generated cards are personal and very attractive.

I have spent a lot of time here in England, looking at cards for brother. The manufacturers have obviously decided that all brothers either smoke pipes, enjoy fishing and golf, or like poor jokes. If the picture on the front is not bad enough, the verse inside would put you off. While the sentiment might be sincere, the ill-chosen words, contrived to rhyme are tripe. You have two choices, either surprise your brother with gushing compliments, or insult him by referring to spreading girth or receding hairline.

I may have to design my own card. It will have to be special as I think I have the best brother in the world. I would not change anything about him, except the bad luck life has handed him. Health wise, he has had more problems that anyone should have to put up with.

It is very difficult to see someone you love endure so many problems. You feel so helpless. What makes my brother special is his dignity and determination. I have never heard him complain or express any bitterness about his lot.

I have noticed that people with major difficulties find strength of spirit to cope. They make less fuss that the rest of us do about quite trivial matters. I did some nursing years ago and was impressed by the courage and cheerfulness of the seriously ill patients, particularly the male ones. Men tend to suffer more silently. That is probably a controversial thing to say, but it is true. Most of my friends preferred working on the

Men's Wards. They were grateful for every small attention; the general optimism and good humour was infectious. Despite the illness, it was a happy working environment.

In the daily course of life I think we have all become less resilient and less resolute. I stopped myself from complaining about the amount of washing I have to do every day ... I recalled my grandmother describing her mother's wash day. The process took up the entire day from filling the wash-tub with buckets of water to manually turning the wringers and pegging it all onto washing-lines. It is shaming to admit but I complain about having to throw everything into machines which wash rinse and dry it all for me.

The washing is only the tip of the ice-berg as I realize how spoiled I have become. Mankind has taken huge steps forward in so many directions, but not in terms of strength of spirit. Our life of ease has made us less resolute and self-reliant.

When you look at life through the ages you realize we all need knowledge, culture, food and inter-action. We basically share the same needs. We satisfy them more easily in the 21st Century. Ancient civilizations created centres of trade and knowledge, produced new ideas in science and art. Literacy flourished; there were advances in geometry, medicine, mathematics and astronomy. All these advances were achieved without technology, air-flights, motor vehicles and so on, and on.

Consider the physical hardships and the length of time required to do everything from administering medicine or producing daily meals to travelling by land or sea. The ethnically diverse populations interacted, prospered and set the course of cosmopolitan life. Their achievements are staggering even today. The different age-old cultures each have a unique way of living and thinking. Whether they will survive is debatable. Adopting the beneficial aspects of the modern world means accepting intrusion which can harm their cultural heritage. The world will be a less interesting place.

Increasingly members of indigenous cultures are affected by the rest of the world. It is a global phenomenon. No doubt one of the hallmarks of this century will be a life more cosmopolitan, more urban and less diverse. We can reach across the world via computer, television and radio, or by cell-phone.

It will be a tragedy if we all live the same way. Despite the world-mass of teenagers wearing their baseball caps backwards, we are different. It's not true that all brothers are pipe-smoking golfers with receding hairlines and it's not true that we are all the same. That's the richness of human life.

Get In Line

If you watch me in a queue, you can see I have lost part of my British identity by the impatient tapping of my toes. Behaving well 'in line' has always been part of British culture. But I have lived abroad for many years and I can't bear standing behind a long line of people.

I glower at innocent shoppers, suspicious of their intent to queue-jump. In a Supermarket I rush to the Express check-out ... the cashier is just locking up their till. Maybe they have been working long hours or simply need to take a break, but at that moment I really hate them.

Either that or I find I am behind the slowest person in the world, who unloads their shopping as if in a trance. This sleepy individual wants to pay by credit card. That's okay ... if they can find it. They turn out every pocket, emptying an alarming array of items on to the conveyor belt. When they start patting themselves, willing the card to appear, I just *know* I'm not going to get out of there in a hurry.

I aisle-hop a lot, moving swiftly from line to line after I've sized-up the number of items in each shopping-trolley. That never works; either some vital piece of cashier equipment goes wrong or a customer wants to pay by cheque. They never have a pen and the cashier can't find hers, so we wait whilst someone in the middle of the queue passes theirs along. Then, as the customer isn't carrying their bank card the cashier can't accept the cheque anyhow. A farce ensues where the customer checks how much cash they have and works out exactly what they *can* purchase. The discarded items have then to be deducted from the previous total. A supervisor is required naturally they are all on coffee-breaks or in-store training. The cashier rings her bell with futile optimism. I fuss and fume. I'm usually quite good-tempered but a queue brings out the worst in me.

If the person in front of me is paying cash, you can be sure they will want to get rid of their loose change. Slowly and methodically, they count out a pile of coins only to find they are a sum short and have to come up with a note – only the coins have to be put away first!

At this point I want to fling my shopping into the air, throttle the person holding me up and leap over the cash point. I don't of course, I wait in line, just as I was taught when I was very young. Some habits die hard.

The British regard the queue as a Social institution a tradition as old as time-keeping. Ask an Englishman to dinner at 8pm and he will arrive promptly and expect you to be ready for him. The British take pride in good time-keeping and they regard themselves as the world's best queuers. It's a source of amusement to the rest of the world. Certainly it's a phenomenon unknown in Europe, where, if you see a queue, you can be sure it's made up of British tourists.

It's a habit other nationalities find incomprehensible. Together with a reluctance to show our feeling and a tendency to lie in the sun at the hottest time of the day, it has earned us a reputation as peculiar or eccentric.

When I lived in Germany I lost the inclination to stand in line. I learned to do as the Germans do; use my elbows. It's not so much a chain-reaction as a pain-reaction. When you feel a jabbing in the ribs you instinctively move aside and that's when people step ahead of you. The only defence is to stand elbows-raised to block the attack. There's no turning back after that, before you know it you are elbow-jabbing with the rest of them.

Italians use a volley of words and trailing arms to secure their position. In France the concept of the queue is totally lacking, which is strange considering the word 'queue' is French!

Along with the various cultural contributions the numerous foreigners who have settled in England have brought about the virtual demise of the queue. It is almost unknown in London. An unruly mob mills around bus stops and cash desks etc. Anyone abiding by the unwritten rules of queuing will be trampled underfoot.

It is the same on the roads. The driving skills of the 21st Century are cutting-in and jumping lights. It's as if people have grown weary of waiting in impeccable order. Older people still do it, but the hectic pace of life and the modern focus on self has brought the queue to an end!

It is a competitive world and achieving success means being first. Being competitive is the fuel to drive change, development and ambition. In some respects it's good that we no longer accept our place (in life). On the other hand the lack of regard for other people is a change for the worse. And where there are 'too many Chiefs and not enough Indians' it's a recipe for disaster.

What's The Problem?

It is often relatively small things which cause us to explode with anger. They are not particularly significant in themselves. It's the sum total of minor irritants which finally cause a breakdown of our equilibrium, or 'cool' as they say these days.

The local Saudi papers and those from England, which I sometimes read are full of accounts of the things which annoy us. Some of them have parallels in each country.

Familiar grouches are lack of service from Government departments, public transport, mobile phones and litter etc. etc.! Most towns and cities have litter bins – in fact there's an abundance of them, so there is no excuse to litter casually. People are often guilty of throwing litter from cars. Apart from being unsightly, it is dangerous when the litter is a discarded drink-can or a cigarette. Cigarette butts are in a class of their own. It's almost as if people imagine that they are biodegradable. They grind them out with their heel in the street in shops and shopping malls. Burning filter tips are tossed into gardens, left on the beaches and sometimes thrown in the path of other pedestrians, or the faces of small children.

Mobile phone users are astonishing. I have one myself; it's very useful, especially as most of the public telephone booths worldwide have been vandalized. But I've yet to 'phone friends or family to inform them that I'm in a supermarket. You cannot help but eavesdrop on these very public calls as you shop. Perhaps other people regard highly the knowledge that their loved one is in the soup and canned vegetable aisle? The most irritating and scary callers though are those who are supposed to be driving. I hate them in restaurants or public meeting and the women who use them (loudly) when we are supposed to be watching our daughters dance. Half the younger generation at least, appear to have their mobile phones surgically attached from the age of ten upwards. I can see the value of them for keeping in touch with parents but I don't believe these youngsters are forever calling their parents. I suppose we should be grateful that they are talking to each other again. I worried about that when they were always playing computer games; side by side, but in total silence – apart from the noise of their games, of course.

I listened to a talented pianist who visited school recently. He played some pieces to our students which expressed his concern at noise pollution. It was interesting to see how they covered their ears or became agitated at some of the sounds which are actually part and parcel of everyday life. A British government study had confirmed what many parents have long suspected – that chemicals used in children's foods and drinks can cause temper tantrums and disruptive behaviour. I don't think it will be long before scientists discover that our current noise-levels have equally undesirable effects.

One of the most maddening hang-ups of modern life must be waiting for an answer from a call centre while being assailed by snatches of music. I think it is supposed to calm us down but it actually makes people angry. They slam down the phone, feeling angry and frustrated. Market research in the UK found that the biggest consumer complaint is the time spent waiting on hold. Almost a third of callers admit to having hung up while left in the queue. A number of British companies have relocated their call centres to India. They save on salary costs, but customers are even less likely to feel they are receiving a personal service, not to mention the number of jobs lost to British nationals!

As to the Service Industry, I could probably write a book of common complaints, so I'll restrict my comments to the disappearance of plumbers and electricians in my home country. Compound-life makes us dependant on maintenance and we may find shortcomings in the system, but you can usually expect someone to fix your lights or toilet, eventually. In England these workmen are thin on the ground, elusive and expensive. In the Yellow Pages, the telephone directory of services, there appear to be thousands of them – literally. But you are more likely to be able to find a media consultant, a life-coach or a crisis-counsellor than you are a plumber or an electrician.

While I appreciate there's more to life than work, I do wonder what all the students streaming out of colleges these days are qualified to do. What happened to technical Colleges where they learned a trade? It seems as if we have a horror of young people getting their hands dirty. What the average householder is looking for is someone who can unblock a U-bend, not someone who can write a thesis on the subject. I'm only half-joking when I say I'll go back to college to train as a plumber. It would be a nice little earner and solve half our domestic problems!

Why Are We Waiting?

I could probably fill this article with expressions about time in the English language. Our international group of friends think we are obsessed with it. Being 'on time' as a desirable objective is one we grow up on. Once it is set in your behaviour pattern it is difficult to escape from. Youth of today find it easier to break the rule ... possibly because they spend so much more time in bed and have to cram everything else into a restricted time span.

Anyhow, my husband and I learned to be on time. We go to work on time and take no more than an hour's lunch-break. We see the start of every show and if we are invited for 'dinner at eight' we'll be there at 8 o'clock. However, the longer we live abroad the more we find the need to change. Having startled more than our fair share of hosts by arriving for a dinner that hasn't even been shopped for, we are learning to delay our arrival. In other words "When in Rome, do as the Romans do".

The problem is, in English social terms, being late can upset or cause strain between you and your friends. They may interpret your poor time keeping as a sign that you don't really want to spend much time with them. Also an English hostess cook will be prepared to serve the meal at the given time. I cannot count the number of occasions I have been forced to serve over-cooked food because the guests came late. And boy, do I mean late! Some nationalities (nameless!) have such a disregard for time that I've either eaten half the meal before they arrive or begun to wonder if they put the wrong date in their diary.

I cannot be relaxed about it; I fuss and fume, constantly turning down the hotplate, stirring the pans and rearranging the cutlery. I'm a nervous wreck by the time they do arrive. I'm also rigid with anger which I mask with a weary smile.

The meal will be barely edible and I resent the time and effort I spent on it.

They do not intend to be rude or to upset me, I know that. They simply have a different concept of time. They are much more relaxed about it. A lot of people don't even start cooking before their guests have gathered. It's smart. At least you get a decent meal, although my appetite is often jaded by the wait. I cannot be the only person in the world who can't focus on a conversation if I'm hungry. The fact that no one else looks nervously towards the kitchen must mean they ate before they came out!

I can appreciate that you can be too early. Just as some people make a habit of being late, others are obsessively early. They arrive at airports hours before they need to, and can be seen waiting outside banks and shops even before they are open. Such people over-value the consequences of being late. You have to get things into perspective.

Most of my countrymen were told as children that it is rude and disrespectful to be late. Poor timekeepers need to realize that people who make a point of being on time can be angered or upset by being kept waiting. If we're ready to meet tardy types half-way, they have to do the same.

Some people in positions of authority seem to enjoy keeping people waiting. Lateness can be a way of showing how relatively unimportant you think an appointment is compared with your other concerns. Colleagues may turn up late for meetings to show how their time is more important than yours. Such people usually have deeply rooted feelings of inadequacy and low self-esteem. It is an arrogance based on insecurity.

It has serious consequences since employees treated this way feel resentful and bitter. They are hardly likely to 'go out on a limb' for their boss. And, in our competitive world, time is money.

Supermodels and larger-than-life celebrities regard being late as an intrinsic part of their 'star quality' to keep their public writing. I can remember a time when it backfired for a famous pop-singer. I was living in Germany and attended a pop concert where the star kept the audience waiting. After two hours almost everyone left; the singer never got her fans back.

Simply, we have to show due concern for each other. It is the only way to get on with people, who are different from us, either in personality or culture.

Speed Limit

We're forever hearing about people who 'live life in the fast lane' these days. These are 'fast' as opposed to 'slow' people. They are often successful people and sometimes very ambitious over-achievers. If they decide on making money they usually exceed their original goal as they are more interested in making money than spending it. Computer Software tycoon Bill Gates, the richest man in the world, was famous for travelling economy class until he splashed out on a private jet last year. No doubt this was purchased to reduce his travelling time. He was ten years old when he first showed his business prowess, successfully hiring out his sister's baseball glove at US $5 a time. Robert Earl who founded the planet Hollywood chain is another workaholic billionaire. They are among innumerable people who find it almost impossible to slow down and relax.

The inspirational world of advertising is currently exhorting us to relax more to indulge ourselves and thus (they imply) improve the quality of our lives. But it doesn't come naturally to some of us. We are genetically programmed to function at a specific speed, so it's pointless to tell someone to 'slow down' if they've been born fast. We're each naturally inclined to function at our own pace.

Fast types are often slim but usually have a voracious appetite. Waking with a mind racing, they get ready for work at lightning speed and race into the day; no wonder their calorie intake is used up. Slow types prepare for the day ahead in a more leisurely way. They tend to chew their food laboriously and allow themselves time to finish a meal. This makes fast types irritable since they set a time limit on everything they do.

I occasionally try to change gear. It can be productive to slow down. I recognize that some of *my* speed is just panic ... I think ahead and the present disappears; it makes time fly too fast. I often spend my day chasing 'lost minutes'. When I make myself slow down I live more for the moment so time slows down. But it's difficult to control myself and I know I annoy friends and family with my constant movement. Thus I was drawn to the theory that certain foods can affect energy levels. Apparently some foods can sap your energy. I thought if I could get plenty of those into my system it would slow me down. It didn't work but in the course of my experiment I came across a number of people who had earnest conversations about food intolerance with me. There are many ways to obsess over food and food allergy is the latest culprit. It's all so vague; there are no reliable tests for food intolerance and physical signs can be inconclusive a lot of sufferers look extremely well. But they appear to be happy to explore every avenue of food elimination. The danger with this latest fad is the risk of people with eating disorders such as bulimia and anorexia masking their illness under the guise of beating suspected food intolerance. Food anxiety is non-gender specific and the unhealthiest person I've ever met was a strict macrobiotic vegan, who in reality saw food as a threat. So I shall continue to eat high speed high energy foods ... but I'll try to do it more slowly!

Given the increasingly rapid rate at which all aspects of the world are changing as we speed towards the millennium, the 'fast metabolizer' is built for the 21st Century. When we need to sort out bigger economic and ecological problems than ever before is there time to hang around?

Maybe not. However, I always do things fast, but I don't always do them well. I always rush to get a task over with, rather than doing it the best way. This makes me unmethodical. I have whims which don't relate to what I should be focusing on and end up with too many jobs at hand but non-completed. I like to read on the move so I can do two things at once and read fast. I also write fast so my writing often looks like something communicated by a spider with ink on its legs.

I like running because it gives me an adrenaline rush. I talk fast and I'm difficult to follow because my mind is on the next subject. At this rate my life is racing past I shall try to keep in mind a saying my Mother keeps in her home "In your haste along the way, take time to look at the flowers".

Must dash ... got to find some flowers.

Hanoi Holiday

A little way ahead of me was an old woman, her shoulders bent forward with the weight of the bag she was carrying. The bag was made of string and there was something moving in it. Intrigued, I followed her into a side street.

This was Hanoi and I knew something strange (to me) was going on. There were a lot of women down this side-street preparing lunch. The Vietnamese enjoy good food and eat three cooked meals a day. Although they are poor, they need to eat heartily because of the hard physical work they do and the ingredients are not too expensive. It is a healthy cuisine based on seafood, chicken and meat, with noodles and vegetables. It is low in fat and easy to digest. It is possible to eat a small banquet for less than US$1 if you eat at food-stalls.

While I was looking at the array of food around the cooks, the old woman squatted with a small group further along the street. I could see the bag gyrating as she spoke and gesticulated. As they talked I moved closer, they were bargaining ... over the price of frogs. The bag contained frogs! I wasn't too surprised since frog's legs are a delicacy of French cuisine and the French had occupied Vietnam for almost a hundred years.

We spent several weeks in Hanoi and like the increasing number of foreign visitors, we were enchanted with the place and the people. We intend to return to Vietnam to explore more of this country of astounding scenic beauty and fascinating culture. After nearly half a century of war and isolation Vietnam has become one of the poorest countries in the world. However, they live with dignity and hope and they are hospitable and friendly. Their grace and beauty is touching and their smiles and warmth affect everyone. Their smiles are contagious; visitors find it a peaceful, pleasant land where values are pure and simple.

Long may it last. The people are untouched by greed or materialism. They are so poor, yet they share what they have generously. They work extremely hard, yet they enjoy a happy social life. The family unit remains strong and united. It is a country of joy despite the economic situation. I felt humbled by their work ethic and their simple pleasure. The economic situation, I felt humbled by their work ethic and their simple pleasures. The economic and social gains of the West in the pursuit of progress had engendered great losses in terms of humanity.

The West is moving in on them, and they need to expand their resources so the cities and beauty-spots are preparing the way, building Western-style hotels, opening fancy restaurants and developing the tourist industry in every way they can. It makes sense; their lives will become less arduous. But I am fearful for them. I am afraid the tourists will rob them of their simplicity and naiveté.

Progress will come and the people will become richer in monetary terms. No doubt they will adopt Anglo-American dress, pop culture, industrial development and so on. They will have more, and they will want more; their simple pleasures and happiness will be gone forever. They will lose more than they gain, but by then they will not remember what they have lost. Now is the time to go there, if you want to see unspoiled landscapes and have people reach out towards you with genuine friendship!

This may be a rather romantic view and does not take into account the toll of their physical labour. As you leave the airport and drive through the countryside, you feel you are in a time-warp. The urban economy is improving much faster than that of the rural areas. Vietnam is now the world's third largest exporter of rice, but most of the country's rice production is achieved without modern agricultural machinery. In the fields peasants labour from daybreak to the setting of the sun.

Back breaking work during seasons which are either steamy hot or wet and cold. No wonder the Vietnamese government fears what China is already experiencing – a mass exodus of rural residents into the already over-crowded cities.

In Hanoi some of the newest buildings were constructed over fifty years ago during the French colonial period and its streets, shaded with lines of trees retain the air of a French provincial town. Despite the poverty, the people are as chic as stylish as any Parisians; they are a handsome people, with charm and grace.

I can't say the same about the traffic! It is noisy and disorderly. The streets are crowded with bicycles, pedicabs and more alarmingly, thousands of motorcycles. These are driven by people of all ages and it's not at all unusual to see a family of four on the same motorcycle. Although I'm used to heavy traffic, I was terrified of crossing the road at first, in the face of this seething mass of motor-bikes. We learned the art by following the local example. You step (bravely!) out into the street and the traffic weaves its way around you. Even on the road the Vietnamese are courteous!

We thoroughly enjoyed our stay. We gained some understanding of the Vietnamese culture, visited historic sites, saw the most famous landmarks and above all, made some friends along the way.

Ah, Yes I Remember It Well

Ask most women about something in their past and they will give you a full account of whom they were with, where they went, even the clothes they were wearing, the music they enjoyed and so on.

A man's recollection would be more concise – precise and lacking in detail. If it was a particularly interesting memory you might get a few more facts. In the main they are more pragmatic – that's the past and they are busy with the present.

The future is something else women like to talk about ... dreams really, about their aspirations in terms of home, family and careers. Obviously these are of concern to men too, but women use different terminology. Men tend to talk about the future in more financial and practical terms.

I wonder why it is that women like to dwell on their dreams and embroider the past. Writers of a certain type have become extremely popular (and rich) because they satisfy women's cravings for fiction in which all the men are handsome and all the women are beautiful, in places where homes are like palaces and everyone appreciates each other.

The appeal of these books is probably related to the escapism they offer. It is a retreat to a more delightful world that the routine, problematic lives we have. In reality most of us have difficult lives. Whether rich or poor, in health or in sickness, we all face challenges. There must be few people in the world who have nothing to worry about, or who are totally content.

Television 'soaps' are as equally popular as romantic fiction. The setting and style of the character differs greatly depending on where the scene is set and the national characteristics of the country producing the series. But the themes are identical.

American shows have people with 'big hair', glamorous clothes and wide smiles. The Mediterranean industry gives us volatile, passionate stars who continually flash their teeth – and their temper. British soaps are more humdrum; lives and homes are less attractive – not very appealing at face value. However, the series are screened worldwide and enjoy enormous popularity.

Whatever the differences between these shows – the soap operas as they were called (now appreciated as 'soaps'), there are similarities. These similarities are the core, the framework to which the writers conform. The shows are a lot like life with all, its joys and problems. But while we might identify with one or other character, we enjoy the fact that they represent other people's lives. Thus they are also a means of entertainment, of escapism.

In most situations and circumstances people are looking towards an escape. They are looking towards something different – and that usually means freedom of some kind.

Marriage guidance experts agree that many marriages do not work because one or both partners entered into it in order to escape the life they were leading. They believe that a wedding can give them entry into a new world. It isn't that simple as everyone takes emotional baggage into a relationship. People do not always change according to circumstance. If they remain at a fixed point, then all the things they disliked about themselves and their lives remain the same.

Disappointment leads to resentment; resentment leads to anger and there you have a recipe for disaster, one sure factor in marriage breakdown is lack of understanding. The gender-differences can be a course of mystery and frustration. Women, in general, don't remember all the words, but it recounts an evening in a couple's past and its obvious the man cannot accurately recall any detail – from what she was wearing to what music they enjoyed, etc. "Ah, yes, I remember it well", he sings, despite forgetting the colour of her gown, and so on.

But what is important is that he remembers the strength of feeling between them, the pleasure of 'togetherness'. Those memories can be an escape route for them both when life is troubling. If you 'escape' together, you run away holding hands – and you can return to life's problems supporting each other. That's really what we all look for in marriage. If you know you'll be supported in all you do then you will dare to do anything. And that is living life to the full.

Commitment and responsibility on the part of both partners is essential if a marriage is to work. It's no good if a woman expects financial support, status and freedom rolled into a neat package. Women need to be sure of their role. It's not about living a comfortable life and having more clothes and holidays. It's about sharing - the good times and the bad. Thus, when you 'remember it well' the most striking memory was that you were in it together.

Celebration

One of my favourite poems for children is 'Eddy and the Birthday'. It was written by Michael Rosen, a family man whose love of children shines through his poetry. Basically the poem is about a two year old who enjoys his birthday so much he wants it again the next day and the next, and so on. It's really funny and every child I've ever read it to has roared with laughter.

Birthdays are a source of pleasure. Small children love all the excitement, the treats, the party, clothes and singing 'Happy Birthday to you'. Come to think of it, these are the same things we adults enjoy! After a certain age the extra years are not welcome, but the celebration is. Like children, we anticipate the occasion.

It is my mother's birthday this month. We are travelling to England to be with her. She's looking forward to having her family altogether. It will actually be a bigger celebration than she realises. My brother and sister have arranged a surprise party for her, to reunite her with family and friends she hasn't seen for a very long time.

I know she is going to love it, just as we have enjoyed the secret. It is so good, when you have grown up, to plan to give your mother a surprise; a treat and a bit of excitement. It is a reversal of roles.

It's also Mothers' Day in England in April, so it's definitely going to be my mother's month! She deserves every bit of attention she gets. She is a wonderful mother.

I match my own mothering skills against hers. Our methods probably vary a little, but the basic needs of children do not change. Children need to be loved and cared for and they need to know how much they are loved. My mother's children have all of that and more.

I suspect that if you asked each of the three of us about our mother, you would probably get different stories. That is because she was three different people at the times each of us was born. No one got the same mother.

Child number one was me. My mother was a young woman living with her husband far from her own family, in a different part of England. Historically, the younger members of a family called upon the older generation for help and advice. As a result of what is called progress, families have moved apart and live in relative isolation. One aspect of modern living is that people often regard the older generation as out of touch. Thus grandparents are the some of the most valuable and least utilised natural resources.

I have never experienced the pull towards my homeland that I have now we have our daughter Jasmine. She adores her grandparents and they have so much to offer in terms of loving attention, wisdom and patience, that she is missing out on.

Anyhow, we will be together on Mother's Day and on my mother's birthday. I often wonder what kind of a mum I am. I can't really answer that. It's like asking me to set my own examination paper and grade it myself.

My mother was endlessly patient and dedicated to staying at home with her offspring. No doubt she was nervous and battled her way through the endless repetitive routine of baby care single-handed. By the time I was four she also had my brother to care for. Most mothers agree it's easier the second time around. For one thing you are more experienced, more philosophical and probably, more worn out! You no longer have the time or energy to overreact. You can measure your progress and problems against what you've known before. So, the second and third child probably have a more relaxed and easy-going mother. And circumstances change. People become richer or poorer, they relocate, they develop in different ways and therefore become different people. That's what I mean when I say the three of us had a 'different' mum.

I have so much admiration for my mother and as I deal with the smallest and most demanding member of our family, that respect grows. Children are certainly the messiest, noisiest and most attention-seeking part of any family. They demand centre-stage position. When there are siblings jockeying for the same position, parents must be hard pressed to keep things equal.

I think the three of us: me, my brother and sister, have always maintained that central position because we are all special to her, and mark significant points of her life. I'm the first-born, my brother is the only son, and my sister is the baby. She's the one who linked the past with the future. My father died when she was young and she links us to him. We got to know him better by seeing him with a young child. She is grown up now, with children of her own, but she will always be the baby. She was the culmination. That's her special place. We all have one and that's what this surprise party is all about ... Happy Birthday Mum – and thank you.

Small Plate, Long Life

I don't buy many magazines. It annoys me to pay good money to look at advertisements which are disproportionate, in number, to the articles featured. I like to look at them in 'waiting-rooms', when I'm going to see the doctor or my dentist. It passes the time and it's interesting to see what the magazine-world is focusing on.

By chance all the magazines I've seen recently have been American and they all shared a pre-occupation with staying young. There are many means to this end it seems, from hormones and oils, to diet and lifestyle.

Understanding how our bodies age has captured the imagination of medical researchers on both sides of the Atlantic. In an attempt to defer old age some twenty million Americans are now taking hormone and food supplements.

We are already living longer. Average life expectancy is ten years more than it was just a few years ago. Better standards of living and general health mean that children born in the year 2000 will have an average life expectancy stretching well into their eighties. Many will live to be a hundred, or more. These predictions are optimistic and do not take into account natural or man-made disasters.

Medical researchers are hoping for more than a natural extension to life. They are taking the view that the aging process is a 'disease' that can be cured. They suggest that in the future we could double our life-span.

I wish they had come up with this a lot earlier. Whereas I'd like to have had double time in my twenties, I don't relish the idea of living twice as long as an old person!

Maybe they are exaggerating. However, there are a number of 'elixirs of youth' being researched. Hormone treatment is a risky business. While oestrogen has been found to promote mental and physical youthfulness to some degree, it may not add years to life.

Adrenal hormones are not such good news since the risks, such as encouraging tumour growth, outweigh the 'feel-good' factors! There are others, hailed as anti-aging cures, but more research needs to be done to satisfy the medical authorities of their effectiveness and safety.

Various oils are said to relieve stress and to mop up the toxins we produce, so they might help people feel better as they grow older.

It is unlikely anyone will enable us to 'turn back the clock'. It is the course of nature, the way we expect things to be. I imagine it would be difficult for a grandchild to relate to a grandparent looking and behaving like a teenager. And how long would it be before people wanted to start over again and begin a new life as a baby?

Well, we can dream and wait for the scientists to come up with the answers, or we can take matters into our own hands. You cannot prevent aging but there are factors which slow the process down. We can take control; improving nutrition and increasing physical activity are good anti-aging remedies.

The physical process of aging seems to be beyond comprehension for some people. Looking to the beauticians, cosmetic surgeons and scientists to provide the means to control it is neither risk-free nor fool-proof. The simple fact is muscle mass declines as we age reducing metabolic rate and energy expenditure.

As I said I get most of my information about the so-called elixirs of youth from American magazines. In the same week I watched a TV programme from America. There is a growing concern among medical authorities about the amount of food being consumed by the nation. The people like to eat out and portions are steadily increasing. The more the better seems to be today's maxim. People cannot resist big portions; they don't even realise just how much they are eating. Served with massive portions it is more difficult to monitor the amount consumed.

Apparently our 'survival genes' which had an important role in early society are working against people. We are generally programmed to eat when there is food. And for many of us, it is all too readily available.

In America people are being supersized into obesity. It's good for business; big portions make big profits, so the trend will probably continue. And people love a bargain. The selling-ploy is 'more food for less money', and value is the key used to entice the population into greed. Judging by the size of people filmed in restaurants for this TV programme, not enough people are questioning the cost to their health.

There is a price to pay. Obesity packs fat around vital organs; they cannot function efficiently. Bones and joints buckle under the excess body-weight. And it looks so gross. No one can deny that a healthy, slim body is far more attractive than one distorted by fat.

It is believed that unhealthy eating habits in children and lack of exercise are going to create serious medical problems in the future – their future. No one would teach a child how to behave badly yet they set a poor example with regard to eating habits. And children 'hold us to ransom' with their demand for fast-food. It's quick and convenient, and it prevents arguments and heartache to give into them. But it's lazy and illogical; we wouldn't allow them to play in a busy road because they *wanted* to.

I read in a newspaper last week that the British consume more chocolate than anyone else in the world. No wonder our children are reported by medical researchers to be the most unhealthy in Europe. I was appalled; it's time to be 'cruel to be kind'. Children aren't capable of devising a healthy diet;

we have to do that for them. If we don't the 'long life' predicted for them will not become a reality.

The Great Divide

Hold all the plans for a new house, a new car and a holiday...
for the next decade. We now have a baby daughter! Thus
blessed, I have paid particular attention to current issues of
gender and equality. Apparently, teachers and academics are
struggling to understand what lies behind the gender divide in
attainment. You can pick a theory, from 'boys don't like
books unless they're about sport' and 'girls are better at
exams'. Whatever the reason, there is a widening gap and girls
are attaining greater achievements than boys.

Much better to say a boy's performance is not as it should
be. It is the teaching methods and the curriculum that should
be addressed. Now girls are outperforming boys we need to
find out *why*, before it becomes a major cause for concern. It
certainly won't help if boys are continually reminded that girls
are doing better.

In the seventies and eighties the education of girls was
under the spotlight, probably for the first time in history in
England. Now the boys are taking centre-stage and we need to
ask how the education system has failed them.

These days we are encouraged to treat boys and girls the
same. In playschools and nurseries, boys play with dolls and
learn to cook. Girls play football and climb trees. There's
nothing wrong with that; children should enjoy the widest
possible range of experiences. But experts are now suggesting
we are interfering with nature – which plays a greater part in
development than many of us have been led to believe.

There are several differences in the structure of men's and
women's brains. The more neuroscientists learn about the
brain, the clearer it becomes that men and women literally
experience different worlds.

The reason girls find it easier to understand conversation
and put their feelings into words is physiological. Boys are
generally more stimulated by objects. They take up more

123

space and are noisier. This is all related to brain differences which have implications at every stage of life.

School is harder for boys to endure at the age of five than girls, who make ideal little pupils. Girls are interested in people, but boys are interested in things. Boys are happier with challenges, taking risks and taking things apart to see how they work.

These days boys and girls follow the same curriculum. But from the first weeks of life it is clear they are different.

Male and female hormones also prime us for our role in life. Boys tend to be more interested in movement than communication. They are also fascinated by the material world. Girls focus on relationships.

In recognition of gender brain differences, a high school in Essex, England, has been testing new methods of teaching boys. Their particular strengths and love of competition were catered for with time – limited projects and regular testing. In just one year the gap in performance between the boys and girls was halved. More schools are starting to employ the same strategies. Theories may come and go; it is action that will bring about change for the better.

Most of us agree equality is fair and good. We are - neither sex - inferior or superior. What we are is different. Every time we ignore that basic premise there is discord.

Unless you've been on another planet for the past couple of years you will know all about the 'Spice Girls' and the attitude that goes with them. It's about girls going all out for whatever they want and getting it. On the surface, it's no bad thing. The grim reality is that girls are trying to be like men. But instead of being assertive they are becoming aggressive. The *truly* empowered stand up for their rights not forgetting the rights of others.

We want equality for our daughter, but do we want her to give up the best bits of feminism to get it? Absolutely not! I wouldn't want to see a return to the days where girls were expected to be 'sugar and spice and all that's nice' and when women were expected to stay at home. We want her to have the freedom to make choices. We don't want her raving about 'girl power', or climbing to success on the back of other people's difficulties. We named her after a fragrant and delicate blossom, but the stem of the plant is strong and tenacious. Our hope is that Jasmine will be as beautiful and resilient as the flower she is named after.

I wonder what the future holds for her. I hope her world will be a place where the individual matters, irrespective of gender, but the scales are rarely evenly balanced. Having received so much attention and made such progress in the latter part of the 20th century the girls may find it's the boy's turn!

A Helping Hand

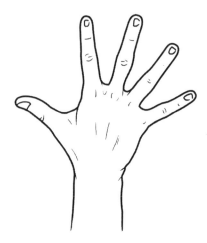

You have to believe in them and support them, no matter what. That's a parent's role. If your child is being bullied you have to step in and help. Conversely, if you suspect your child is a bully and determined to parade their power in front of their peers then one must deal with their nastiness, making it clear it is intolerable cruelty.

Socially, children are driven by a need to belong. Exclusion is something they fear most. The misfit or scapegoat in a group is often the target of cruelty. Few children or adults can stand up to this onslaught of social cruelty.

Schools can never stop exclusion and teasing entirely. But a school must have a moral code that rejects it. Teachers can work to combat it by using cooperation and collaboration methods in the classroom. Children encouraged to work together tend to accept each other and unpopular children gain wider acceptance within this situation.

I read a report by an American sociologist recently, which said that children are becoming increasingly violent towards each other. The ultimate crime, of course, has been committed – on more than one occasion in America and recently in Germany, where disturbed children took the lives of their peers and some of their teachers. What they see in the world is extreme violence. Adults also openly engaged in angry exchanges – even over simple things, like a parking space. The internet, television and movie-world also show 'the tough getting tougher'.

Children learn by example, so they need to see adults behaving responsibly. If they see us being friendly and avoiding gossip, put-downs and exclusion, it is a good start. Children recover quickly from many social upsets that might leave an adult feeling resentful. Once we are sure an incident is a childish spat and not a case of bullying, then we have to let them 'forgive and forget'.

Adults need to know when to withdraw and let their children sort things out for themselves. We can easily undermine their friendships by imposing adult concepts of justice. We could all take a helping hand from our children in terms of friendship and how to rescue them!

'No' is Just a Two-Letter Word

I often wonder why the word 'no' sticks in the throat, for so many of us. It doesn't matter what the circumstances are, or how little we want to get involved with something, we just can't say no. I have always thought that it is a characteristic of people of a certain temperament. Some people would call it a flaw of nature, because it indicates a lack of assertiveness or self-confidence. People who cannot say no tend to be helpful and good natured. But they don't always feel that way. Often they feel angry – at their weakness and at other people's thoughtlessness.

They are the sort of people who are always prepared to help out, and they usually respond willingly. However, if the demands continue endlessly and there are not reciprocal favours, people naturally started to feel 'used' and taken for granted. It's an uncomfortable feeling because there is an underlying concern that one is being taken for a fool.

Recently, I realised that there is another reason for lack of assertiveness. I have always been quite fortunate, it seems, although I have experienced what it feels like to be treated indifferently. However, I was very shocked to hear that a woman of my acquaintance cannot use the word 'no' for fear of being beaten. I will let her remain anonymous for her protection.

She was born and raised in a country where the extended family is not a joy, but a burden. Helping each other is not a decision but an obligation. Thus they are victims of their culture.

In brief, this woman has a slightly larger apartment than her husband's relatives. Thus they visit, uninvited, every weekend, staying there from Wednesday night to Saturday morning. They bring with them neither food nor drink. The 'hostess' spends their small savings and uses all her 'free' time to provide them with food, morning, noon, and night.

The size of the problem is indicated by the fact they all manage to consume ten kilos of rice, as well as the food that goes with it.

Apart from lack of subsistence from the visitors, neither help nor gratitude is forthcoming. The other women in the family leave her to prepare, cook and clear-up unaided. It is X who is left to do the laundry after they leave on Saturday. All she can expect is criticism – either the food could be improved, increased in quantity or maybe the dessert wasn't to their taste. Whatever the reason, she can always expect criticism.

It is a depressing state of affairs, and entertaining so many people so often is exhausting. It is also a financial drain on these poor hosts. But when I said I thought she should say that they are welcome once a month, but not every week, I didn't expect the reaction I got. She said she couldn't say 'no' to them because her husband would beat her.

I hadn't expected that. It just goes to show how naïve, and how fortunate, I am. My husband would never ask or expect me to act as an unpaid cook and servant – not to his family nor anyone else in the world. I do complain about various things at times – probably more often than I ought. My meeting with X will make me think twice before I do.

But thinking that 'I can't help what I am', can be an emotional opt-out. Our minds are capable of adapting to new ways of thinking. Our emotions are too. Given these facts we should be able to stop worrying about what other people think and stop doing things just because we think we should.

I once attended an assertiveness training course. The word 'should' was banned. It is the favourite word of the 'overwhelmed', we were taught. When I find myself using it now I try to think again and ask myself why. If it is only because I think something is expected of me I try to free myself from the 'should shackles'.

At least I have the right to say no, and the freedom to say it. I will reflect on this. It's just a two-letter word in the English language, but it is a mighty one.

Fire! Fire!

I was trying to read my small daughter a story about three bears living in a wood. Every time we came to a page with a picture of a tree on it, she closed the book. She didn't answer when I asked, "Why are you doing that?" or when I enquired whether she liked the story or not.

Eventually she started to say, "Fire" and "Dangerous."

"Where's the danger?! I asked.

"In there," she replied, pointing to the lounge.

I have become adept at translating her words and signs, and realised she was referring to the television. The news programme had carried video footage of fire for a couple of days ... the forest fires in America and then the fiery fireworks first at the Dutch pyrotechnic factory, which devastated much of the town of Enschede, and a few days later, the explosion at a factory near Valencia.

The causes of the explosions have not yet been revealed. There are a number of possibilities, from chemical reaction to human error or carelessness. But the blast sent a fireball through the town of Enschede, destroying much of it. A large number of people were killed or seriously injured in both factory explosions.

It seems that neither disaster could have occurred under normal circumstances. From various reports it is apparent that the materials in the factories were stores in a negligent way. Whatever the cause, the fact is that many people lost their lives and hundreds of others lost their homes.

The pictures on the TV screen were horrifying; no wonder they were still in my daughter's mind. Etched into my memory are the forest fires of Athens in 1995. We were visiting Athens at that time. From our hotel room we watched the blaze and listened on the TV to the reporters at the scene. It was devastating to watch people flee from their houses or search for their loved ones, or cry for the loss of their homes and the memories and memorabilia they held. Horror turned to disbelief later as some angry citizens told us the fires had been set deliberately. Apparently, while there are trees growing on the land in Greece, it cannot be developed. Setting fire to the trees was an easy way of getting rid of the problem. The actual cause of the fire was purported to be a carelessly dropped cigarette end. It is open to speculation whether or not the cigarette was dropped on purpose. Arson was never proved, but the land has never been replanted with trees. I think that speaks for itself.

There are innumerable fires which mysteriously occur in old buildings or failing businesses. Sometimes the owners collect the insurance money; sometimes they are caught out and get a prison sentence instead.

It's a very nasty and risky thing to do since fire is notoriously difficult to control. Fire has been a symbol of cleansing and of life through the ages. People usually learn this is something they cannot take control of. However, in 1997 during the dry season in Indonesia landowners attempted to clear the vast areas of forest for their plantations. But thousands and thousands of square miles of land burned in a round of fires which blazed beyond control and created one of the world's greatest environmental disasters.

Pollution created many problems from medical complaints, loss of tourism, ruined crops and a food shortage, to the clouds of smoke, which were also blown to Malaysia creating a choking haze.

Slash and burn agriculture has been practiced in tropical countries for centuries for subsistence but with little effect on Nature. However, this was a widescale operation with forests torched to clear the land for commerce. Official propaganda tried to lay the blame on the shoulders of small farmers and the effect of El Niño which held back the monsoons giving good conditions for burning. In truth, it was the giant agricultural businesses that torched the land. Fire is free, and it often bursts out of control – so by accident or design the plantations may be expanded that much faster.

Wealthy entrepreneurs, with money in mind, ravaged the rain forest and spread a pall of air pollution throughout Southeast Asia.

There have been more fires, both in areas where they continued to smoulder and in new locations, since 1997. Cycles of fires of this magnitude will affect both human and animal life in the region, upset the ecosystem and destroy one of the world's last remaining tropical rainforests.

People who play with fire, get burned. Man is creating an environmental nightmare.

The Art of Deception

'Hey, Watermelon Man', the tune of this song plays in my head every time I open the refrigerator. What meets my eyes is a pinkish, thick-skinned meanly fleshed watermelon … a very distant relation to the vivid, luscious sample on display at the trader's roadside pitch. Those tantalising slices were surely sweet and soft, temptingly moist and juicy.

They were a great advertisement for his wares; they drew the attention of every passing motorist. It made one's mouth water; nothing like a thirst-quenching watermelon on a steamy day in Jeddah.

I usually buy a half of one from one of the large supermarkets where I can see how ripe and choice it is. I don't know anything about this tapping business; I don't know what I'm listening for. So I play safe and see what I'm getting before I buy.

Last Thursday however, my eyes roved over the enticing mounds at the roadside as we passed seller after seller … some traders alert and watchful, others reclining in the shade or fast asleep. It intrigues me that merchants selling the same thing cluster together. I would think the competition too great. It is also exceedingly irritating to pass so many in one space and them before you've made up your mind to buy, you pass by the conglomeration and there are no more – no last chance to buy!

On this occasion we pulled into the slip-road in time. I got out and strode purposely towards the vendor. He looked at me with little interest and wearily lifted the first melon to hand. Propped up on the banks of melons were huge chunks of a melon he had cut. I was wary, I've had unfortunate experiences with less than red melons before, just like the one in the 'fridge' right now in fact.

Before I voiced my questions I knew, instinctively, that he'd tell me it was sweet and red. He must have developed xray vision throughout years of experience, he seemed so sure. I'm still uncertain; I proffer fifteen riyals which he snatched with such alacrity I knew I'd paid too much. But he had pocketed the money and it was too late to barter.

I'm annoyed with myself; I thought I was so smart, but I was no match for him. As we drove away he looked up slightly and I saw a gleam of triumph in his eyes. I feel foolish. That amount of money is not important, but my pride is.

I'm even more annoyed when I get home and cut through the green skin. No juice runs down the sides of the green rind. The melon is dry in texture and insipid in colour. Not only is it tasteless, I've paid over the odds for it. Well, it was my own fault. I can hardly blame the vendor for taking the price *I* set!

I close the door on my folly after I have taken out eggs and milk from the 'fridge'. I assemble everything I need to make my husband some pancakes (sort of thick crêpes). I take the packet mix which I bought in the UK, for convenience sake 'just add an egg' is printed in large red letters on the front. The manufacturer omits to say you have also to add milk and a little salt.

As I am beating the mixture with a fork I mentally compose a list of all the ingredients required to produce home-made pancakes – an egg, milk, salt and some flour – wait a minute, I have added everything to the mix I bought apart from the flour. I have paid three times the price of a kilo of flour for a few grammes. I can't be alone in the purchase of this product. A fortune is being made from flour in a fancy bag. I have been deceived by glossy packaging.

I've only myself to blame. I did not take the time to read the list of ingredients on that packet. That is the whole point of convenience foods, to save you time – but at what a cost!

Paying More For Less

One of the biggest loads of nonsense I've ever read appeared in a magazine under the guise of a fashion expert's advice. It invited us to join the increasing numbers of celebrities who are dedicated followers of 'dressing down'.

This is an 'effortlessly stylish' (quote) way of dressing; so casual the neighbours will think you are popping out to buy a carton of milk when you go out. It is not to be confused with the 'grunge' fashion associated with second-hand and torn or worn clothes. But it is equally contrived. The idea is to appear in a state of disarray which is purported to be slightly androgynous, yet curiously feminine. Really?

Do some women really believe such guff? Most of us enjoy dressing-up; it's something we do from a very early age. Our daughter is under two years and she loves handbags and beads, wears hand cream, perfume and has definite ideas about her clothes. I haven't taught her any of these things; I haven't encouraged her to wear my fanciest shoes. The ones with flat heels are neglected in favour of the stylishly-heeled pairs. She is doing 'what comes naturally'.

Apparently, if you 'dress down' there is nothing to distract the eye. Nothing to catch the eye more like, which is what ladies like to do. Why on earth do these fashion 'experts' think women used berries to stain their lips and kohl to enhance their eyes centuries ago? Certainly it was not in effort to be insignificant or self-effacing.

The surprising thing about the new 'dressing down' trend is that it is designers who support the fashion. They say it is nothing new; it is symptomatic of certain celebrity-personalities. They are 'laid back', deliberately casual. Some celebrities in the 60's appeared in public this way. Thirty years on the young elite perpetuate the fashion. I'm probably old-fashioned but my reaction to media coverage of these stars is one of disbelief. I cannot imagine why anyone so rich and famous would want to look as if they had grabbed 'any old thing' to wear and rushed out without even combing their hair.

How designers have become involved is mystifying. The clothes they dress their models in look as if they have come from a downtown market and shabby boutique in a run-down city. This 'simple' look could be achieved by purchasing a couple of mismatched pieces of apparel and wearing them un-ironed and wrinkled.

Perhaps it is no coincidence that designers who dress down the most successfully are women. Why would they want to put young, attractive females into unobtrusive clothes, in quiet colours which aim for anonymity begs a question.

I don't believe any of these young stars are in the public eye, both on screen and in society, because they want to remain anonymous! But some are similar in one way; they appear to want to snub the very public which make them famous.

It seems they 'dress down' to let us know they couldn't care less what we think of them. The designers who had fed this 'statement' are smart indeed ... to give less for more.

The clothing is costly. They fork out a fortune to look as if they haven't tried at all. Once, designer-buyers demanded visible value for their money ... a logo here, a signature motif there. Now there is none of that; it's all understated Jilly B or Anna Fu or whoever.

Sometimes you get to see these style-gurus, these lady-designers of the new century. They appear at the end of their latest fashion show and could easily be confused with the stage-hands or even the lavatory attendant. That sounds very cynical, but I'm wary of those of my own gender who contrive to make the 'beautiful people' appear ordinary.

Some of them are not so beautiful without the elaborate make-up and clothing we associate with the film industry. But we don't want to see them looking like the rest of us do when we get up and pull on 'house dress'. They come from a fantasy world which we enjoy because it transports us from the flat and ordinary aspects of life. It is great to enjoy someone else's glamour and to appreciate the effort they have gone to. If I want to see women in disarray, in jeans or oversized shirts and skirts I can look down any European high street and observe who has given up, without paying a fortune to do so!

The Sands of Time

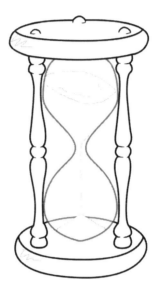

Several of the local newspapers recently carried articles about plans to extend tourism in Saudi Arabia. They said that holiday visas will soon become more easily available. The visa is an obvious priority and then Saudi travel and tour guides should be trained so that visitors can get the most out of their visit.

The airfare will deter casual travellers looking for little more than beaches and entertainment. Visitors will be well-heeled, very curious about the Middle East and no doubt, interested in history. They will be happy with a busy itinerary. They will have plenty to spend and demand upmarket hotels, want to try local cuisine and take home local art works.

There's a vast market out there of well-educated, middle-class people who will respect Saudi customs and do nothing to compromise local social norms.

It is natural that people should be curious about the Kingdom – a land that seems to have it all; breathtaking landscapes, a rich cultural heritage, cities with amazing architecture, intriguing old cities and modern ones. Whether haggling for trinkets in the Balad, or strolling in the air-conditioned *souks*, people will be spoiled for choice. You can buy almost anything there – and they will want to buy … gifts souvenirs and bargains. I would advise tourists to travel with an almost empty suitcase and fill it here!

I'm not sure when people would come. In the summer even the Saudis, who are used to the heat, tend to travel to escape the inferno of June, July and August. Still, there are people who would enjoy a hot climate for a short time. They have every opportunity to cool off in the hotels, restaurants and retail worlds or a beach resort area. Beach cabins and villas in Obhur and the North shore offer facilities which vary from Spartan simplicity to complex centres with swimming pools, sports facilities and restaurants.

People can indulge in water sports. Sailors together with snorkelers and scuba divers can enjoy one of the world's richest coral reefs and shallow coastal waters. Or you can laze about, or gather with friends, to enjoy a bit of peace and tranquillity.

Somehow the sheer intensity of the heat adds to the mystery; the uniqueness and strangeness. Because of the ease and growth of modern day travel some places and countries have become so familiar they no longer attract the avid travellers eager to explore new worlds.

T E Lawrence was involved in the Arab revolt against the Ottoman Empire in the early 1900's. After this young British officer had fought alongside the Arabs, the Middle East became a focus of interest for ordinary people, as well as the military and government. Lawrence became a romanticised figure. As a 'man of letters' he wrote 'The Seven Pillars of Wisdom' and many other works which show how he embraced the ways of the Arab World and revealed his gift for observing and assimilating new cultures.

One can only speculate on his reaction to Jeddah and the desert lands as they are now. The sun never seems to set for most people. The transformation of the land is astonishing. The desert started to bloom long before the invasion of high-tech modernity. The 'people of the desert' are not going through irreversible transformation. It is development and progress and its success is reflected in buildings, road networks, trade and some aspects of social life. It is history repeating itself, but in a new and tumultuous way.

The lands of the desert have attracted all kinds of people for centuries. Many things have changed. Wealth inevitably imposes change on tradition and culture. But there are still influxes of foreigners who seek work and the opportunity to observe a new land in the making.

The desert will always attract and entice people irrespective of their race or culture. Its beauty is raw and serene. Craggy massifs offer an invitation to climb, a place to view the rocky skyline, the untamed land, which used to stretch as far as the eye can see. You feel so small, so insignificant in the face of such natural splendour.

It is splendid, amazing; the isolation is awesome. The place exudes mystery and it touches some part of you, bringing to you peace and stillness.

Nowadays, the sheer distances that have to be crossed in order to escape men and machines have ended spontaneous visits to the desert. You need to plan your route more carefully and carry more supplies. You need to get away from the havoc Man is wreaking there.

Recently we were in an area familiar to us some years ago. It was unrecognisable. The number of trucks travelling back and forth to dump waste were countless. Ceaselessly churning the dust, polluting the atmosphere, breaking up roads, they journeyed into the desert to destroy the environment. No thought appears to be given to the long-term effects of this dumping. The painstakingly cultivated farms and trees are grey and choked, already beyond help. The natural life that was created there has been destroyed. It is a terrible sight.

It is not a solitary incident and disregard to our planet is widespread. All over the world, Mankind, who once sustained life in harsh and uncompromising environments irreversibly tamed their habitat and now seem intent on destroying it.

Sun Block

We visited England last month to see family and friends. The weather was appalling most of the time. I had expected rain – April showers and all that. But I was not prepared for the wet snow we call sleet, not hailstones and frosty mornings. It was miserably wet and cold. The grey skies were gloomy and depressing. It didn't help to know that the weather had been 'glorious' as everyone said before we arrived.

English people love to talk about the weather. It is a daily topic of conversion, probably because there are climatic changes within hours sometimes. There was a kind of excitement at the sudden cold spell.

I've forgotten what it is like to wrap oneself in a raincoat and get on with the routine of household tasks. Things like walking to the shops, car cleaning or worse, gardening, are no longer part of my life. Now is continuous rain and dark, dreary days. Climate has an amazing effect on one's daily routine.

It also affects moods. Most people are more cheerful and optimistic when the sun shines. Even British reserve diminishes. The summers have been good in my home country for the past few years. People have enjoyed the opportunity to get outdoors and enjoy the fresh air and the sunshine.

When the weather is warm life is much simpler too. Unless they have spent any length of time in colder climes people from hot countries cannot appreciate how much the weather affects the quality of one's life.

Apart from feeling horribly cold, we were irritated at having to abandon our outdoor plans. For example, we wanted to take our daughter to parks, boating lakes and the zoo. None of those things would have been pleasurable in the pouring rain.

Instead, we headed for the shopping malls where herds of people gathered. The attraction was shelter, not shopping. We soon became tired of it. In any case, there are more shops than one could dream of in Jeddah, and we like to spend our holidays doing something different from usual. We were lucky to have plenty of friends and family to visit or the holiday would have been a disaster.

When you live in England you become accustomed to postponing things until the weather improves. It's a trait we have lost and I am temperamentally unsuited to uncertainty. I hate it when my intentions are subject to some outside force such as the weather; I like to be in control.

Another irritation was getting dressed! English people dress for the weather. That means wearing layers and layers of clothes when it is cold. Being muffled up to the chin is fine when you are outside. However, once inside people's homes or the shops, where there is central heating, you are forced into peeling off those layers because it is so *hot*. It is exhausting putting on and pulling off clothes all the time. It is also inconvenient because you are eventually carrying more clothes than you are wearing indoors.

I can appreciate the objective. Providing warmth when it is cold outside ensures people linger longer. While they are sheltering they will probably buy something. But I cannot imagine why shops have to be so oppressively warm. Even the sales assistants, who were obviously not wearing coats, were uncomfortable. Apart from that, the heating bills must be extremely expensive. I expect that the cost is met by the retail price. I would prefer things to be cooler and cheaper!

We did have a few sunny days and they made such a difference to the way we felt and it was a joy to be outside in the fresh air. Now we have returned to Jeddah and there is plenty of sunshine. But the heat is intense already and one has to take precautions. Being fair skinned we are at risk from over-exposure to the sun's rays. I feel as if I've been caught between a rock and a hard place. In England it was too wet and cold to go out much; here it is too hot for us.

I am grateful for air-conditioning. I admire people from temperate climates who lived and worked overseas without it, years ago, I don't think I could have coped. But maybe I could. It is only in recent years that we have all become spoiled and self-indulgent. We now complain about many difficulties which we would have taken in our stride previously. We have adapted to our life of relative ease.

It will be interesting to see how Europeans adapt to the ever increasing temperatures induced by global warming. I expect homes will change somewhat. No doubt people will have fans and air-conditioning. Eating habits will probably change too. And after the initial euphoria of getting a suntan at home people will rush to purchase things to protect them from the sun. Perhaps it would be prudent to invest in a sunhat factory or a sun cream company!

Different Planets

I read a book once which suggested that men and women come from different planets. The whole point of the book – I think – was that if we imagine this is the case we would come a lot closer to understanding each other. I don't think so!

We are walking around with very different brains, men and women. They were perfect for when women stayed close to the home weaving, gardening and caring for the children while men roamed around hunting for dinner. They are not so wonderful for these days of paternal leave, women pilots and the like. The problem being that no matter how efficient people may be in role-reversal nothing will change a person's natural inclination.

There is none such creature as an absolutely typical male or a typical female. There are great variations and it makes life more interesting. We are all more than a box of brain cells, but the brain is the organ through which we understand the world. What we now know about the brain – the fundamental differences in male and female form – strikes at the very heart of equal-opportunities feminism.

For those of us who have always enjoyed being female and have never wanted to jostle with men for stress – at the top jobs, science is on our side. We are neither inferior nor superior; we are different.

I don't think many men at work think about what to have for dinner; a lot of women do, we exchange ideas and make shopping lists in our breaks. Men notice dinner-on-table or dinner-not-on-table, but rarely share women's attention to detail, be it the sight of dust on the furniture or the matching cloth and serviettes.

A man with an 'unfortunate haircut' wouldn't dream of staying at home until it grows. Try coaxing an unhappy woman who thinks her hair looks a mess, out of doors. It's a no-win situation I can assure you I cannot imagine any man either going home to change, or hiding in the bathroom, if he discovered someone was wearing the same suit as he was. There are countless women whose evenings have been ruined buy such an event. Men shop when they *need* to; women shop because they like to and they will always find they need something to wear.

Behind the scenes, pre-outings, you can always find a woman anguishing over what to wear … long or short, flamboyant or simply classic, jacket or shawl, heels or flats, sandals or court shoes, endless agonising decisions. Whereas a man chooses a suit. Suits are universal and ubiquitous, a symbol of manliness. There's no getting away from it a man's suit is an enviably splendid garment.

Right now it's trendy to use biological determinism as an excuse for men's domestic shortcomings. With washing up it's cups yes, pans no. With vacuuming it's the centre of the room only; anything requiring at attachment is ignored. Take cleaning the bathroom for another instance, tiles and taps will gleam, anything below eye-level will cause him problems.

It's a similar thing with the washing machine. I know women are supposed to be more versatile with language than men, but would it be really difficult to learn, what 'woolmark' means? You have to resort to wearing synthetics when a man is in charge of the laundry because it's boil, wash, or perish. But for every man willing to have a go, there are a hundred mechanically-minded males who profess not to know how a washing machine works!

Things mechanical on four wheels, on the other hand, tend to throw women into a state of frenzy. I confess to being unable to reverse into a parking space, change a wheel or locate the engine. And you might just as well hold a road map inside-out and upside-down for all the sense it makes to me.

Since we've all been forced into making quasi-public presentations for work, I've been struck by how much better men present themselves and their ideas. For all our predisposition for articulating our feelings and thoughts, public speaking strikes a woman with terror. I've lost count of the times I have watched confident, amusing, well-adjusted women suffer dreadful misery. It does not take a rowdy or hostile audience to do this. Even a roomful of supportive friends or colleagues can bring on this terror. I've had this experience many times. I try to take my husband's advice; prepare everything carefully, give them something to smile at and to try to force myself to believe they like me. But I'm always so scared I fix my gaze away from the people, to some corner of the room, so I cannot see if anyone looks bored or quizzical, or in any way judgemental. When it's over I return to being articulate, voluble and confident. I've never seen a man panic when the flip-chart falls off the easel, or stop mid-sentence and gaze into space, dumbstruck.

I've heard women say they can read their men like a book. They can't, because they can only interpret things from a woman's eye view. I can enjoy a meal without having to know what the ingredients are and I don't need to know what 'makes a man tick'. Vive la difference, I say!

What's In A Name?

When a woman gets married in England it is usual for her to take her husband's family name after the ceremony. She keeps her first names but changes her surname. From Barbara Steel I became Barbara Knowles. I know this is not the custom here, or in many other countries, where you keep your father's name for life.

This is gaining favour in England now. Women choose to keep their family name and add their husband's name to it. Thus, Miss Green will become Mrs Green-Black for example. Alternatively women will retain their family name in the workplace for professional reasons.

Two family names linked by hyphen (-) used to be a status symbol. People with what is known as a double-barrelled name were perceived to be 'upper-class'. Since we have become a meritorious and multi-racial country 'class' is less significant though snobbishness lingers. There are still people who consider themselves superior to others. They are not all English either!

First names create all sorts of problems when people are about to acquire a new generation. Then out come the name-choosing books. Members of the family also add their own suggestions. A lot of consideration is given to the choice, but it still can leave children with names they will loathe.

Many people detest their names, at least until late in life, when they sink into a sort of weary resignation. The trouble with first names is that they come with a lot of social, historical and personal baggage.

Nothing fixes you more firmly in time and space than your name. As the years pass new generations find the names of their parents, aunts and uncles, outdated and odd. Some of today's time bomb names will cause people to explode with laughter in the future.

Nowadays we laugh at Agnes, Madge, Alfred, Cuthbert or Doris. Fifteen years on people will laugh at Yvonne, Michelle and Roger or Eric. No doubt exotic sounding names which are popular now will make people smile as the beautiful young Jade and so on becomes sixty-something.

Fashion in names is as eccentric and unpredictable as hemlines. They come in waves, unseen at the time, but all too apparent as the years slip by. We thought we had chosen well when we named our daughter Jasmine, pleasingly unusual and evocative of the lovely flower. So it is, but it's becoming very popular. *It's a lovely name*, however, and suits her. It may be a problem if we return to England and she goes to school and finds she shares her name with half the female population of the same age.

One of the consistent truths is that, for girls, most names end in 'a' are upmarket. Arabella, Georgina, Tara, all persuade people that they are indelibly linked to the upper class.

Sharons and their equally dated brothers Wayne and Darren have gone into the dustbin of history. But thirty years ago some parents sitting down with the 'Names Book' must have thought they were splendid names. Some names just fade away and sink into oblivion. But what is confusing is that fashion is cyclical. Names that were apparently long gone with ancient aunts and uncles have begun to appear on the births column of *The Times* newspaper. Anyone called Albert these days must be either six months or 85 years old, there's nothing in between.

It's a safe name. Strangely enough many of the Kings and Queens of England, William, John, Henry, Mary, Elizabeth are inoffensive. That is probably all you can ask of a name.

My brother John seems happy enough with his, although there was some confusion in the family when I married another John. We resolved it by my referring to them as 'our John' (brother) and 'my John' (husband). My sister on the other hand dislikes her name and modifies it. It is ironic since I passionately wanted to be called Annette. However, I don't have a problem with 'Barbara'. I quite like it and I was named after my mother's sister who is a delightful person.

Probably the main reason people cite for disliking their name is that it evokes unpleasant imagery. They don't feel their name reflects their character and so they jettison them or truncate them. All the Mo's (Maureen), Sam's (Samantha), Ben's (Benjamin) and Joe's (Joseph) of my acquaintance are people who are, at least; a little unhappy with the full-length original.

Middle names can be dropped or hidden under an anonymous initial. But schoolmates will always unearth it. I remember my friend Susan M Turner never knew a day of teasing until it was revealed that the 'M' name was Maude. Beware of initials, I still remember the torment of a little boy I taught years ago. Did his parents not realise that Brian Anthony David Boye would be carrying a schoolbag and class name of 'BAD BOYE'? It was enough to scar him for life. A name like that must have put a brake on ambition. No matter how clever he is, no 'BAD BOYE' is going to become Prime Minister!

Time To Pause

I read a health magazine recently which had a section about relaxation and finding some peace in this frantic world of ours. It caught my attention immediately. I often feel I cannot squeeze any time to relax into my daily schedule.

It never ceases to perplex me that, in an age where so many devices and services have been developed to make life easier, our primary challenge is having too much to do.

The complexities of life increase with each passing year. Everything happens too fast and we cram more and more into our lives. Scientific and technological developments should mean we have more free time. Instead, we face almost endless lists of things to do while juggling careers, family life, social and recreational interests. We think we can cope, but the overload grows leaving us stressed and irritated.

There comes a time when you have to cut things out and leave room only for the priorities. Otherwise all the things we take on board stop us enjoying life.

Travelling by car used to be a time of respite. Now I have a small child beside me I've become a mobile-entertainer. And, whether or not it is because my daughter is with me and my senses are heightened, it seems there is more dangerous and discourteous behaviour on the roads than ever. You cannot have peace of mind while the cars around you weave from lane to lane – and to ours.

Home is always busy with people coming and going, tasks to do, meals to serve. If you add a background noise of machinery (washing machines, dishwashers, vacuum cleaners, etc) the television and general household noises you have a stress-inducing atmosphere. Together with the never-ending list of things to do it is almost impossible to escape.

Finding the opportunity to be alone in these circumstances is almost impossible. I know a lot of people seek refuge in the bathroom. Water therapy is renowned for de-stressing but it is the personal space that can give the greatest benefits.

The magazine article I referred to carried a report about a new book called *Stopping, How To Be Still When You Have To Keep Going*. The writer believes that our complex lives lead us into a situation where we continually add to chores, responsibilities and other pursuits until we no longer function properly. Life loses its sparkle. We become jaded and no longer do anything very well or with any delight. There is something about life today that makes us feel we have to keep going.

I don't know why this is; why we have the urge to keep busy all the time, to compete, to improve our lives, ourselves. Perhaps it has something to do with the role-models presented by magazines and mass media. We are presented with images of perfection which many people feel they must strive to imitate.

We cram things into our lives and cut things out which might be desirable but we feel we cannot make time for. When things get too much for us we refuse to acknowledge the cause – we are doing too much.

Dr David Kundtz who wrote the book I have mentioned believes we all need to 'stop' for a definite period. It means doing literally nothing or a short time, or an extended period – say for a week or a month. During this time you focus your attention inwards and bring to mind the things that are most important to you and then you smile. This will relax and re-motivate you.

It isn't enough to slow down because the world is speeding up all the time. Dr Kundtz believes we should make a decision while the world keeps turning. It will continue to turn. I can recall a number of occasions where I have kept to an overloaded schedule because I believed my input was indispensable. But when I have been forced to stop because I just couldn't go on (human frailty), I found life went on without me; people coped and night turned into day without my influence!

It took me a long time to learn a lesson from this. It is a salutary one; none of us is as important as we think. We are simply a part of the whole.

Even death cannot stop the wheels of time. While the loss of a loved one is devastating, people do find the will to go on and they create a new way of living and cope with their loss.

So we can all find time to be still if we wish, if we are determined to do so. It is part of the harmonic balance of life. Just as we suffer if we overload on potentially stressful activities.

We have to make time for ourselves. With all our knowledge of mankind and what makes us tick to hand, it is ironic that personal mental survival has become something we feel guilty about. So … I'm going to create a few pauses in my life, I know it will help me live it to the full.

Family 2000: A Never-Ending Story

I rarely read a newspaper from cover to cover. I know a lot of people read every detail, but I scan the pages until I find an article that seems relevant to me and my life. It is an insular outlook and one which mainly pertains to the female of the species! This I was attracted to an article in a local paper written by a Saudi lady reporter about the role of women in the year 2000. With the new millennium in mind, she encouraged the ladies of the land to develop a more global outlook. Since technology enables us to communicate with every corner of the earth, it is time, she wrote, to reach out to the rest of the World. Women should not use circumstance or situation as an excuse to be 'set' in the family environment. Even people who do not wish to leave their home can use the internet, for example, to make discoveries and broaden their outlook.

Personal development is most desirable. We become dull when we are stuck in a 'time-warp', when we know nothing more than we did when we left school. I had a lot of empathy with the reporter; it is time some of us became more up-to-date with the technological developments happening around us. I find them astonishing, but with some effort, I could understand them, and make use of the opportunities they afford, in terms of time-management and efficiency, at the very least.

My personal '20th Century Mentality' is due to laziness mixed with the lack of opportunity for hands-on experience. There is probably an element of fear attached since we are all wary of things we do not understand. Also I am unmotivated, since I don't need the knowledge at work right now, and I have no desire to send or receive e-mail.

We have been dubbed 'the dinosaurs', people like me who have not kept up with technological development. My excuses so far run from being busy with a baby, living overseas, and waiting for the new millennium, to sorting out family problems.

The latter reason is probably the most honest and significant. The article I mentioned at the beginning ended on a positive note, reminding women that our role in the family is of paramount importance. I support that whole-heartedly; my family is a joy and a job for me. Looking after a family brings plenty of satisfaction and pleasure. But the endless routine of it all is sometimes irksome. At times you feel isolated from the rest of the world. Time squeezes you into a narrow band of thinking and re-active behaviour. It's good to mentally step outside that area every now and then.

An expression from the English language I like very much is, 'You can't see the wood for the trees'. It means that we get so caught up with things that don't really matter, that the more important things elude us. It happens to me sometimes and I try to stop it. It could happen in the daily grind of chores, shopping, feeding the family. You can become so 'busy' you forget to stop and enjoy the pleasures of being with your family.

I have friends of many different nationalities. While our cultures may differ we all agree that family life is what matters to us most. In the new millennium, the structure of the family as we have known it may change. Working mothers, marriage breakdown and families separated by career opportunities abroad are some issues which face families all over the world.

Times change and things move on. There was never a golden age of the family because each generation has had problems to deal with. Health and hunger don't feature so heavily in the modern world but there are many families under a lot more stress in the modern world in a way they weren't when I was growing up. The traditional family unit has changed, but however different it may be, family life is still at the heart of most communities. Most people find the stress of juggling the demands of work and family the biggest problem they face.

Economically, it seems imperative that more women work, but I wonder if that is simply because we want more material things. I have talked to a number of expatriate women who were working mothers before they joined their husbands overseas. They all admitted they assuaged their guilt at not spending sufficient time with their children by buying them gifts all the time when they went out to work.

Everyone I spoke to agreed; the greatest benefit they enjoyed, living away from their home country, was the joy of family life. Having escaped the frantic pace of life in our home countries, we can enjoy our freedom to focus on the family. The benefits and the problems created by working mothers will soon be experienced in Saudi Arabia on a much greater scale. Let us hope the prospect of mothers being *expected* to work does not occur here, either in the year 2000 or beyond. Certainly we now have a *choice* although that right is subject to circumstances and economics. In reality the mother who would choose to let someone else bring up her children is second rate. Nurturing a basic female instinct: it's what we do best!

Working At Home

By chance, I kept bumping into the family of an Egyptian boy I taught a couple of years ago. We all live in Jeddah, but it is in London that we accidentally meet. We usually have a sort of parent-teacher consultation, but it's not a problem since I rate their son almost as highly as they do.

I once met them in the middle of Oxford Street when I returned, on a whim, to the shop I'd just left, my long-suffering husband muttering about my indecision. And, right outside, in the midst of the hub-bub of this bustling city, was the family of one of my pupils. He was dumbfounded, whether it was the horror of seeing a teacher while on holiday, or sheer surprise, I'm not sure: Probably a mixture of both emotions.

More recently we met at Heathrow Airport as we boarded the plane to Jeddah I hadn't seen them for a very long time and they expressed regret that I was no longer teaching - until

I told them about my daughter that is. Then they were full of approval that I'd decided to 'stay at home' with her.

I haven't actually *stopped* teaching; I just don't do it in school anymore. Every day I am encouraging, motivating and guiding our daughter ... teaching, in fact. I had intended to return to my job since she was six months old but circumstances dictated otherwise.

I am more than happy with the outcome. This is the job I want, bringing her up myself. I hadn't expected to feel like this. I thought I wouldn't have to change if I didn't want to. I'd just be the same, but plus a baby.

In fact, there were many changes, and I feel I've acquired a whole new identity. These days for many modern mothers there is a big adjustment from careers and personal development to motherhood. It's not a side issue; it infiltrates every aspect of your life and personality. Instinct seems to take over from intellect. It was reasonable to assume I would continue my career. In the event I was unprepared for the overwhelming desire to spend every minute of the day with her.

The day goes amazingly quickly and I have a sense of pride and achievement at the end of it. I probably have a tendency to babble on about every minute detail of it. I suppose this is a deep-rooted need to prove I'm actually doing something busy and important all day.

I know I'm doing the most important thing on earth. Sometimes other people need convincing. It's hard to put it into words; it just *feels* right.

Anyhow, I still find time to do lots of different things for myself. When she sleeps I exercise and I write. When I first started writing I used to sit at my desk and work undisturbed. It's a bit different now. But the hard work of writing is thinking. Thoughts have to emerge, they can't be forced. You need time to daydream, to let the imagination wander in order to be productive. I actually enjoy a lot more daydreaming time now I've had a baby who likes to sleep in my arms.

A lot of good sentences come with the nearness of sleep. I keep a pad beside the bed in case I wake up with a good idea or have an interesting thought just as I'm going to sleep. It would be gone by the morning. In any case, the idea of forgetting it would keep me awake, so I write it down.

We still travel and Jasmine enjoys lots of outings and expeditions. Children learn a lot from everyday life. In fact more and more parents are turning to home study. They are educating their children at home, either from circumstance or dissatisfaction with the learning process in schools today.

From a personal and professional view I read about the World-Wide Education Home-School Company. It offers assistance to parents working abroad and to home educators. A year's curriculum is individually selected for your child and advice and support and regular assessment is offered.

The impetus to home education, and the methods used are varied. The number of families involved is increasing rapidly. In America, one and a half million families educate their children at home; all the evidence points to impressive results with home learners often two years ahead of their peers.

You have to enjoy your child's company and the level of concentration is tiring. You need plenty of energy and enthusiasm and to be inspired by the belief that this is the best choice for your child. It might seem isolating, but with a certain amount of effort, that can be overcome. Socialisation is not an issue; children educated at home mix equally well as those educated at school.

The article certainly set me thinking about the future. In particular I was struck by the findings of a professor of education in relation to the number of questions children ask. Before they start school they ask a fantastic (inexhaustible) number of questions. When they first go to school, they are still asking about 30 questions an hour, but, within a year that is down to about four questions. This this hardly surprising when you consider the teacher might have to field that many questions from any number of children in the class.

These facts give me food for thought personally both from a professional and a mother's point of view ... In brief: Do I listen enough to the children I teach? And, am I going to educate my daughter at home? I've got a few years to think about it!

Our Choice

Breakfast time had become a bit of a challenge to me. A 'battle of wills', is probably a more accurate description. It involved my daughter and I, and what she would or would not eat.

A while ago the truth dawned on me; I was offering her too many choices.

She would make her choice and then, before I could even finish preparing it, change her mind. No doubt she had in mind the many possibilities I had offered.

She probably felt she was missing out by opting for just one. So I would prepare fruit, put jam or honey onto bread, cook oatmeal-porridge and offer bowls of cereal and she would refuse the lot!

I needed to find a more rational approach; I've become very reactive since our daughter appeared on the scene. I tend to run about like a headless chicken at times. Whatever she wants, she wants it now and that included the multi-choice breakfast menu. I couldn't keep up with it.

Aside from the morning's frenzy of feeding, bathing and dressing, I took 'time out' to consider the problem. I couldn't recall such a struggle over breakfast when I was a child and neither could my husband. It didn't take long to realise why: We weren't given a choice. Following the generation of this era, we will have the Y-generation who cannot make a decision in the face of so many choices. I'm taking steps to limit Jasmine's right now! Life was made simpler for Mums with the advent of cereals, corn-flakes, rice crispies, etc, which you place in a bowl and pour milk over. You serve food and drink all in one bowl. Easy!

Of course, you can lead a horse to water, but you cannot make it drink. I've lost count of the number of mornings Jasmine sits and stares at a bowl of cereal.

I can't help but think of the millions of children worldwide who are starving. They wouldn't play with their food. Hunger may become a wider issue in the future.

Improvements in agriculture have kept food supplies high enough to meet the growing world's demands. However, in spite of this, many people go hungry because we haven't learned to share. I was astonished to read a while ago that 30 million Americans, mostly elderly or children, rely on charity for support or they go hungry. Despite the country's wealth, they have to choose whether to pay the rent or buy food. It's quite an indictment of society today.

A time may come when increasing numbers of people go hungry. At many points in history it has been predicted that the world would soon become over-populated. Famine would be worldwide. So far, these predictions have been wrong.

However, these days better health and diet have cut the death-rate. More babies survive and we live longer. The world population steadily rises.

Earth is a finite place with room for a finite number of people. The simple truth cannot be changed by man, no matter what improvements are made regarding food production and habitation. A daily increase of almost a quarter of a million people, added to the billions alive today, makes it certain we are headed for trouble on a gargantuan scale.

Our fragile, over-extended planet has two problems to address. One, to ensure the planet can produce enough to feed the billions who will be born in the future. Secondly, if we do manage to produce enough, the issue is distribution. Will we have the means and the will to distribute food to all those who need it? Today, farms worldwide produce enough to feed everyone. But hundreds of millions cannot afford a balanced diet. As the ever-increasing population competes for food, rising prices may leave many more hungry in the future. The problem is not production but distribution. Local food supply has little to do with natural conditions. Some people who live in fertile lands are hungry. Others, such as the Japanese, do not have sufficient land to grow their own food, yet they are well fed.

A major reason for this disparity between the 'haves' and 'have nots' is politics. Some of the world's governments do not have the will to assure their people the basic elements of food supply. At this moment in time, war rages in countries where people are starving to death. The cost of the weaponry would go a long way to buying food for their own people.

They will wait for aid from across the world. They will obstruct and deter those transporting food to those in need. They give many of their countrymen a death-sentence since relief will not arrive in time.

War, famine and disease may well sort out the population explosion. It seems terrible that we choose not to do it for ourselves. In view of all that man can achieve, it is tragic.

Diminishing Wonders of our World

Wherever I am, if I mention living in Jeddah, someone will make remarks about the Coral Reef here; it is certainly one of the Wonders of the World. I had my first opportunity to snorkel here and I will never forget the magnificence of the underwater world. It may be one of the most beautiful things in creation.

I do not like being in sea water, but I managed to overcome my phobia in order to experience the pleasures described to me by other snorkelers and divers. I cannot believe I will ever learn to dive, but who knows? My time here is not yet over; I may surprise myself.

The article in a recent *Variety* supplement 'The Undiscovered Red Sea' was very interesting. The diver-writer, Frank Fields, reminded us that popular dive sites around Jeddah are severely degraded. He had to travel a long way to find an untouched area of the sea. I hope most divers will find the journey to the location of his trip too far away. It would be a tragedy if new areas were ruined.

Coral reefs rival the rain forests in diversity of life. But they are under environmental stress and are at risk from over-fishing, pollution and disease. We know that rain forests are vanishing fast. The coral realms are collapsing one after another. In just the past few decades one-tenth of the Earth's coral reefs have been destroyed. The remaining coral is becoming so seriously degraded that scientists warn that three-quarters could lie in ruins within 50 years.

The speed of the demise of the coral reefs is all the more shocking when we bear in mind that many of these structures have been around for 50 million years or more.

Tropical countries find snorkelers and divers a vital source of income. But the reasons for keeping coral healthy extend well beyond the tourist industry. Since reef fish make up a large percentage of the global fish catch; together with other reef foods they support millions of people. So the survival of whole cultures is at stake.

Hundreds of millions of people live in coastal regions. In the tropics one-third of those coasts are associated with coral reefs which protect the land from storms and daily erosion. Reef fish also provide food for ocean dwelling fish. The food chain means Man will eventually suffer because of decreasing numbers of commercial fish.

Coral also influences ocean chemistry and affects carbon dioxide levels in the atmosphere. Thus it influences the health of the Planet as a whole.

Medical research has found that some coral organisms yield compounds active against such health problems, as asthma, heart disease, leukaemia, tumours, fungal infections and viruses. Therefore, there may be many more cures and treatments to be discovered. The coral reefs are of amazing value apart from their beauty.

Coral reef limestone can be cut into masonry to provide homes and other buildings. It provided building materials for houses in the old city of Jeddah. When crushed it is a major ingredient of cement. Like marble, it can be transformed into a works of art. It is a work of art – Nature's art, we have to cherish it.

Climatic extremes, increase in water temperature, pollution, over-fishing, industrial toxins, the destruction of forest and landscapes, signal the pressures that modern populations are placing on the Earth.

Environmental protection is in Man's best interest. There is so much more to discover about the natural world. But we will have destroyed large parts of it before we appreciate it. A large percentage of medicines come from nature or from chemical formulas found in nature. Exciting and life-saving discoveries have been made recently to cancer which is one of the most feared diseases of our era. Medicines made from Pacific yew trees and from deep-sea sponges hold hope for millions of cancer victims. We should be working to preserve the ecosystem not destroying it in our pursuit of materialism.

All habitats depend on humanity's willingness to protect the life that's left.

The ecosystem is taken for granted. It has no market value, so their long term protection is often ignored. Humans damage the ecosystem extensively, yet they are essential to human existence.

We are a self-centred species. But it is a great conceit to imagine we can exist independently. Every living thing is interrelated. Man is only part of the natural web of life. We are part of the whole. We need to develop a new way of thinking or our species will also become extinct.

For other species no decision will change their fate; they are simply doomed to disappear from Earth. We can determine our fate by saving the Planet, thereby saving mankind.

Man has always accepted a challenge; this may be the greatest one of all.